HURRICANE
SEASON

HURRICANE SEASON

THE UNFORGETTABLE STORY OF THE 2017

HOUSTON ASTROS

AND THE RESILIENCE OF A CITY

JOE HOLLEY

hachette
BOOKS

NEW YORK   BOSTON

Hachette Books
Hachette Book Group
1290 Avenue of the Americas
New York, NY 10104
hachettebooks.com
twitter.com/hachettebooks

First Edition: May 2018

Hachette Books is a division of Hachette Book Group, Inc.

The Hachette Books name and logo are trademarks of Hachette Book Group, Inc.

The publisher is not responsible for websites (or their content) that
are not owned by the publisher.

The Hachette Speakers Bureau provides a wide range of authors for speaking
events. To find out more, go to www.hachettespeakersbureau.com
or call (866) 376-6591.

Library of Congress Control Number: 2018932207

ISBNs: 978-0-316-48524-1 (hardcover), 978-0-316-48525-8 (ebook)

Printed in the United States of America

LSC-H

10 9 8 7 6 5 4 3 2 1

For Houston

Yeah, this is a rainy day in ol' Houston...

—BLUES MUSICIAN SAM "LIGHTNIN'" HOPKINS, 1961

CONTENTS

PROLOGUE

In downtown Houston on a balmy November night, thousands of loud, exuberant baseball fans are surging along Texas Avenue and into the hulking monolith called Minute Maid Park, home of the newly crowned American League champion Houston Astros. Clad in orange jerseys and blue caps and carrying homemade signs scrawled over in Sharpie—"ALTUVE: MVP," "HOUSTON STRONG"—many are taking a break from long hours replacing drywall or laying hardwood floors or trying to sponge away mold. Just weeks earlier, a brutal hurricane dropped more than 50 inches of torrential rain on greater Houston over a four-day period. The storm, with the quaint name of Harvey, would destroy or damage tens of thousands of homes and upend the lives of countless people in the nation's fourth-largest city.

Tonight, however, these fans are pouring into Minute Maid Park to a different kind of history being made. They will stay on their feet until the last out. The roar they're generating inside the closed-roof stadium is as loud as Hurricane Harvey thunder. They're here, they're loud, they're ready—even though the seventh and deciding game of the 2017 World Series is unfolding before their eyes, not in Minute Maid Park but in Dodger Stadium in Los Angeles, 1,500 miles away.

In their one and only prior appearance in the World Series, the Astros had been swept by the Chicago White Sox in four games in 2005. Now, for the first time in the 56-year history of the franchise, the Astros are nine innings away from a world championship. If few fans could make the trip to LA to watch their heroes take on the National League champion Dodgers, they can't get much closer than watching the game on El Grande, the 54-foot-tall, 124-foot-wide high-definition screen in center field. Perhaps they imagine the racket they are making can somehow carry westward on a mighty wind and Altuve and Correa and Springer and Bregman and all the other Astros they have cheered all season can take heart from Major League Baseball's loudest fanatics, their noise magnified by a retractable roof Astros players always want closed. The players insist they feed off the noise.

As baseball fans—and maybe even non-baseball fans caught up in the Astros' splendid story—know by now, the Astros defeated the Dodgers in seven games, the final one played in the storied hollow of Chavez Ravine in front of 54,000 hostile fans. No one left either stadium that night—November 1, 2017—until José Altuve, the Astros' mighty-mite second baseman—the American League's Most Valuable Player—fielded a routine ground ball and threw to first base 3 hours and 37 minutes after "Play Ball."

For the Astros, the combination of a magnificently played series, a 101-victory regular season, and a crippling natural disaster back home was so incredible it might have given the schmaltziest Hollywood screenwriter pause, but those fans filling Minute Maid saw it. They believed. It happened. And the fourth-largest city in the nation, a city still reeling in the wake of disaster, could smile, could celebrate, could ask bleary-eyed coworkers the next morning, "How 'bout them Astros?!"

"This season, this team, and this World Series has left Astros fans addled," the *Houston Chronicle* reported the morning after the championship. "From Beaumont to Corpus, Brenham to Fairfield, they awoke Thursday morning and pinched themselves. *We won the World Series*. The Houston Independent School District closed Friday for a victory parade downtown. With an expected attendance of 750,000, it will likely surpass those that celebrated the end of World War II."

The Astros' first-ever World Series victory is a baseball story, to be sure, but it's so much more than that. It's the story of a major American city—a city (and a state) that the rest of the nation doesn't always love or understand—winning Americans' hearts because of its grace and goodwill in response to pain and hardship. Houston has endured its share of storms and hurricanes over the years, but nothing like Hurricane Harvey and the ensuing flood, the costliest natural disaster in American history.

It's the story of a team of likeable, refreshingly good-natured guys who each wore a "Houston Strong" patch on their jerseys and meant it. When Houston was down, they picked the city up and carried it. They brought hope during a dark time. It took a special mix of personality and panache to do what they did.

Sportswriter Richard Justice described the Astros as "a nearly perfect mix of youth and experience, passion and resolve." Dave Sheinin of the *Washington Post* was impressed by what he described as "the deep sense of humanity they all seem to possess," from pitcher Charlie Morton's "self-discovery" to Carlos

Beltrán's "quiet leadership" to Altuve's "infectious joy" to George Springer's "profound grasp of this team's role in its city's recovery."

In their close and intimate connection to the Bayou City, the modern-day Astros resembled storied teams of old. They were a modern-day version of the '50s-era Brooklyn Dodgers, when Duke Snider and Carl Furillo and Gil Hodges strolled along Flatbush Avenue, stopped in for a loaf of bread and a bottle of milk at the corner deli and chatted with shop owners. Houston may be a massive, diverse metropolis disguised as a sprawling suburb, but it likes its local heroes when they're familiar, accessible, open, and hardworking—guys like Bum Phillips or Earl Campbell, Nolan Ryan or Craig Biggio. These Astros certainly qualified, whether it was third baseman Alex Bregman hanging out with fans at Pluckers Wing Bar or pitcher Lance McCullers Jr. helping rescue dogs "who have been thrown a curveball by life." Bregman, McCullers, and all their teammates had shared their city's trauma during Harvey.

In the closing weeks of the 2017 baseball season, the relationship between suffering city and successful team became symbiotic. "It kind of became something that we rallied around," McCullers said, weeks after Harvey. "We still have pictures hanging in our lockers. It's still something we think about, because people here are hardworking people, and they went through something that a lot of people can't understand. A lot of people lost everything. So for us to be able to just play baseball for a couple of hours and for those people to be able to have a little bit of joy, to get away from what they were having to go through is pretty special, to be able to give that to them."

It's hard to exaggerate the fury and devastation Hurricane

Harvey unleashed upon Houston and much of the Texas Gulf Coast. Beginning on a Saturday night in August, Houstonians in houses small and large, in modest working-class neighborhoods and in sprawling estates on the forested banks of Buffalo Bayou, stood at doors and windows and watched it rain, watched torrents of rain come down relentlessly, the noise like a train coursing through the neighborhood. As rising water invaded yards and then burst through doors, walls, and electrical sockets, Houstonians retreated to upper floors or attics or clambered in the dark onto wet, slippery roofs. They waited. The rain kept falling.

Those who could helped rescue their neighbors. Houstonians heard later about the Iraqi refugee who ferried children through a flooded neighborhood on his inflatable dinghy. We heard about the football coach in a Houston suburb who overloaded his fishing boat with evacuees. We heard about the "Dreamer" in another Houston suburb who barely slept for days as he helped rescue people as part of an emergency medical team on an ambulance.

Vast neighborhoods were under water for days, tens of thousands of homes were made unlivable. Houstonians spent days dragging stinking, water-heavy belongings—or what had been belongings—out to the curb. They called tow trucks to come take their ruined vehicles away. They filled out paperwork. They wept.

Eighty-eight people died in Texas. The storm and the even more devastating flood left in their wake nearly $200 billion in damages. Houston and much of southeast Texas will be a long time coming back.

The Houston Astros were leading their division, the American League West, when the hurricane hit. The 'Stros could have been irrelevant, no matter how well they were playing, but that's not how it turned out. In the midst of crisis, the team understood—and so did their fans—that the game—the national pastime—they played so well meant something. Like the New Orleans Saints after Hurricane Katrina and the Boston Red Sox after the Boston Marathon bombing, the Astros were playing for their devastated city, and as fate would have it, they won a World Series. They were known as a team wedded to analytics and data-driven decisions, but number crunching can't explain everything.

"We care what happens to the Astros, when we choose to identify with them, because we know exactly how hard it is to get a win when you need it most," Dan Solomon wrote in *Texas Monthly*. "And after the hurricane and the flood and the aftermath, Houston absolutely needed a win. An Astros World Series win doesn't clear the mold out of someone's house, or restore their lost belongings, or put a roof over anyone's head. But it tells us that difficult things are possible, no matter how stacked the odds seem."

"This is a dream come true," an ebullient Springer told reporters in the Dodger Stadium locker room after Game 7 of the World Series. "That 'Houston' on our chests means a lot. They have endured a lot. We're coming home a champion, Houston!"

Carlos Correa, the Astros' enormously gifted young shortstop, kept a photo in his locker of a Houston woman trudging through fetid water up to her knees toward a rescue boat idling in what had been her front yard. "That photo's at eye level," Correa told a reporter. "Whenever I have a bad day, whenever I think about throwing my glove into my locker because of something that happened to me, I look at that photo and realize I have nothing to complain about."

The tall and graceful Correa, the American League Rookie of

the Year in 2015, was one of several uncommonly gifted athletes the Astros' vaunted analytics approach—think *Moneyball*—had uncovered in recent years. That list included Springer, a powerful slugger and rangy outfielder; Bregman, whose Brooks Robinson–like defensive play at third base and his clutch hitting in the World Series, made him a plausible choice for MVP had Springer's bat not come alive; and, of course, the stubby and tenacious Altuve, three-time American League batting champ, and not only the MVP but also the heart and soul of the team. The extremely talented young-sters played with a youthful exuberance that was infectious, per-haps explaining in part why the vanquished Dodgers took out a full-page ad in the *Houston Chronicle* congratulating the Astros on their championship.

However precisely moneyball measures character, it seemed obvious that the Astros front office had signed good guys. Fans identified with them. They appreciated their enthusiasm, whether it was Altuve and Correa executing their trademark leaping pir-ouette when one of them scored a run, their mod neo-mohawk haircuts, or unabashed right fielder Josh Reddick's locker-room strip show—down to a red, white, and blue Speedo—after big vic-tories. Fans loved it when Correa dropped to one knee on national TV and asked his girlfriend to marry him a few minutes after he and his teammates had vanquished the Dodgers. It was right in character.

Another point of identification: the Astros reflected the diver-sity of the city they represented, the most diverse city in America. The first baseman was Cuban, the second baseman Venezuelan, the shortstop Puerto Rican, the third basemen Jewish New Mexi-can, and the catcher a southerner from Georgia. In the summer of

2017, they were all Houstonians—Houstonians who came through when their adopted city was in need.

"Every year we ask the city and the fan base to rally around the team," Astros manager A. J. Hinch told the *Chronicle*. "It's OK for a fan base to ask the team to rally around them."

Maybe Springer, a young man who has conquered stuttering, said it best: "To bring the city something that I believe they desperately needed, they desperately wanted, and desperately deserved is one of the best feelings in the world."

Bill Brown, the Astros' longtime TV announcer, has calculated that in the history of Major League Baseball in Houston, the original Colt .45s and the Astros had gone through more than 850 players and 22 managers, including interim managers. "It took 56 seasons and 9,023 games to get to this point," he noted in 2017.

In a hurricane season unlike any the Bayou City had ever endured, here's how it happened.

CHAPTER 1

Hottest Game in Town

DODGERS LEAD SERIES, 1-0

They had two big swings, we had one.

ASTROS MANAGER A. J. HINCH

On October 24, 2017, opening day for the 113th World Series in Major League Baseball history, Los Angeles was hot enough to make a mockery of the old label "Fall Classic." For LA's first World Series in 29 seasons, it was desert-summer hot, *Day of the Locust* hot, so hot that Ed McMahon, Johnny Carson's perennial sidekick on the old *Tonight Show* might have stumped his boss with the venerable setup question "How hot *was* it?"

How about this for an answer? So hot that egg-frying sidewalks were unnecessary; infield grass was skillet-hot enough, maybe even for eggs and bacon.

In palm-fringed and picturesque Dodger Stadium it was 103 degrees, the most blistering World Series game-time temperature in history. LA shattered the previous record, set in 2001 when the Arizona Diamondbacks welcomed the New York Yankees to Phoenix, where it was a comparably chilly 94 degrees. (The coldest in recent years was in Cleveland, when the Indians hosted the Florida Marlins in the '97 Series. For Game 1, it was 35 degrees. And snowing.)

As fans seeking shade filtered in a couple of hours before game time, a pregame pitchman—just like on *The Tonight Show*—worked to whip up enthusiasm. A giant American flag rippled across the outfield. A sound system worthy of a Christina Aguilera concert extravaganza blasted out "Let's Go Dodgers!" Later, the familiar faces of LA celebrities—Dustin Hoffman, Jerry Seinfeld, part-owner Magic Johnson, Jason Bateman, Lady Gaga—flashed across two jumbotrons. The celebs were on hand to watch their Dodgers claim their first World Series rings since 1988, when masterful Orel Hershiser dominated the powerful Oakland A's and gimpy-legged Kirk Gibson hit an iconic home run. Nearly three decades was a long time.

Washington Post sportswriter Dave Sheinin observed that when "gospel singer Keith Williams Jr. belted out the national anthem, the sweat stain on the back of his suit jacket grew from the approximate shape of Vermont at 'Oh say can you see' to that of Idaho by 'home of the brave.'"

For more than 54,000 sweltering fans in LA, most of them wearing Dodgers blue—with maybe a thousand orange-clad Astros fans in their midst—Sunset Boulevard traffic was more of a bother than the heat. They loved their Dodgers, winners of 104 games. They could stand the heat.

Nor did the temperature seem to bother Dodgers starting pitcher Clayton Kershaw, a Dallas native accustomed to games played under a withering Texas sun. The tall Texan wore a heavy

Dodger warm-up jacket as he loosened up in the outfield before the game.

"They're from Houston, I'm from Texas; it's going to be hot for everybody," he had said the day before. "We're all used to it. It will be fine."

Kershaw, who at 29 was born the same year the Dodgers last won the World Series, was his generation's Sandy Koufax, except bigger. At six feet four inches and 228 pounds, he overpowered hitters and had compiled a career record of 144–64, with a scintillating career ERA of .236. Every year he was a favorite to win the Cy Young Award and had done so three times. In 2017, he was 18–4, with an ERA of .231, despite missing several weeks with a back injury.

The Astros were well aware of the future Hall of Famer's abilities; so was Dave Roberts, his manager.

"I think the fans get cheated on not getting the opportunity to see him in between starts," Roberts told reporters. "Because… to be behind the scenes and to watch him work so diligently, with detail, every single day, that's something that, for me, I marvel at.…I wouldn't know what it's like to be a superstar. But with what he does every single day, with working with a purpose, with everything he does, it makes sense."

For all the individual honors he had won, this would be Kershaw's first World Series appearance—and he would be facing the team with the best sticks in the majors. The Astros finished the regular season with the highest batting average, highest on-base percentage, and highest slugging percentage. They also struck out fewer times than any other team. And they were prepared. The *Los*

Angeles Times reported that the Dodgers pre-Series scouting meetings stretched into the wee hours of several mornings.

"It's the best lineup that we've seen all year," Manager Roberts told reporters. "There's so many ways they can beat you."

The Astros, playing in only their second World Series in team history—the only team to represent two different leagues in their two appearances—had vanquished the Boston Red Sox and the New York Yankees (winners, by the way, of 27 world championships). They were young but unintimidated. Whether the heat would bother them was an open question. It gets searingly hot and humid in Houston, to be sure, but the Astros play under a retractable roof, in an air-conditioned building.

Astros leadoff hitter George Springer, unlike the traditional leadoff, is basically a cleanup hitter with the power to beat you with one swing. He represents a trend that caught on in 2016, when teams like the Cubs with Kyle Schwarber and the Indians with Carlos Santana started using their designated hitters to lead off. As Hunter Atkins of the *Houston Chronicle* pointed out, "These men are built like nightclub bouncers, not base stealers. They get paid millions to cross home plate, not reach first base."

Springer is six feet three inches and 215, so he's no Nellie Fox either, but the big-man trend worked for the Astros throughout the regular season. When Springer leads off with a home run, "there's an energy boost in our dugout," Hinch said. He hit 34 in all.

In LA against Kershaw he didn't lead off with a home run; most hitters don't. He fouled off the first pitch, a 94-mile-per-hour fastball. With his trademark hesitation windup from a relief pitcher's set position—an unorthodox pitching motion that keeps the hitter off balance and allows Kershaw to hide the ball until the last possible moment before release—the Dodgers left-hander finished off the Astros' young center fielder in four pitches, the third strike a devastating slider that veered downward toward Springer's feet.

Alex Bregman, the Astros' young third baseman, flied to left, and second baseman José Altuve grounded out to shortstop to end the top half of the inning. As the Astros went down 1-2-3, Kershaw threw just nine pitches, seven of them strikes.

Starting for the Astros was Dallas Keuchel, a dependable precision pitcher and the 2015 Cy Young Award winner. That was the year the bearded Oklahoman went 20–8 with three complete games and a 2.48 ERA. The left-hander led all American League pitchers in wins and was the starting AL pitcher in the 2015 All-Star Game. He pitched with shoulder pain throughout the '16 season—"I sucked," he said—and finished with a 9–12 record and a 4.55 ERA. In 2017, Keuchel rediscovered his form, going 14–5, with a .290 ERA—despite an undisclosed injury to his left foot the second half of the season.

Only three Dodgers had ever faced Keuchel. One was center fielder Chris Taylor. Keuchel retired him three times in 2014, two years before the Dodgers acquired Taylor from Seattle, before the outfielder revamped his swing and blossomed into a slugger.

The first pitch Keuchel threw to Taylor was as juicy as a rib eye at Wolfgang Puck's CUT restaurant on Wilshire. An 88-mile-per-hour fastball straight down the middle was a rare Keuchel mistake, and Taylor took advantage. He smashed the pitch deep into the left field pavilion, an estimated 447 feet away. Suddenly, shockingly, the Dodgers were on the board.

Manager Roberts had told the Dodgers before the game to be
sluggers, not just hitters. Get it into the air, he was saying, because
the ball would carry farther in the searing heat. Taylor merely followed instructions. His blast was the fourth leadoff home run in
the history of World Series opening games.

After that first unfortunate pitch, the Astros' bearded ace went
on to strike out third baseman Justin Turner on seven pitches, got
rookie first baseman Cody Bellinger to ground out to second, and
right fielder Yasiel Puig—the flamboyant and excitable fellow with
the Dodger-blue mohawk haircut under his batting helmet—to
ground out to short. Eleven Keuchel pitches and the inning was
over. One of those 11 Keuchel would love to have had back.

Returning to the mound with an early lead, Kershaw started
off the second by retiring shortstop Carlos Correa on a fly ball to
center field. He caught Yuli Gurriel looking as a 94-mile-per-hour
fastball streaked by and then got catcher Brian McCann to ground
out to second baseman Logan Forsythe, who had shifted into shallow right field to play the odds against the pull hitter, batting from
the left side. It was another easy inning for the Dodgers ace.

His Astros counterpart gave up a single to Kike Hernández to
open the bottom half of the second, but got Corey Seager to ground
into an easy double play to end the threat. Forsythe popped out to
center.

After Kershaw started the third inning with another called
strike three, this one to Marwin Gonzalez, the Astros got their first
hit of the game. Josh Reddick, a former Dodger who went 0-for-22
in the postseason before his first hit in the American League
Championship Series, smashed a hard grounder that darted just
beyond Bellinger's glove. But Kershaw stayed in control, striking

out Keuchel on a futile effort to bunt and then Springer, up for the second time.

The leadoff hitter for the Dodgers got on base for the third consecutive inning, as Austin Barnes hit a grounder through the infield into shallow left for a single. Kershaw laid down a perfect bunt, sending Barnes to second and Taylor to the plate. The man who started the game with a home run on the first pitch hit a rope to shortstop Correa, who ended the inning by doubling Barnes off second.

In the top of the fourth, the Astros finally broke through. Bregman, a recent LSU star, hammered a Kershaw fastball over the left-center field fence, tying the game at one run a piece, and becoming the youngest American League player to hit a home run in the World Series since Manny Ramirez for Cleveland against Atlanta in 1995. Both were 23, but Ramirez was 60 days younger when he slapped a pitch out of the park.

Bregman, one of a few hitters in the Astros' lineup who had never faced Kershaw, said the pitcher's deceptive delivery, with its pause at the top and a strange stutter step—a way for his arm to catch up with his body—was nearly impossible to prepare for.

"Honestly, you can look at all the video you want. But until you get in the box against somebody, you don't really know what their stuff looks like out of their hand," Bregman told reporters. "You kind of had to sync up everything with that [pause]. Towards the end of game, I think we got a little more synced up."

Kershaw then got Altuve and Correa on called strikes and paralyzed Gurriel on another unhittable slider. It was Kershaw's eighth strikeout against the team with the least strikeouts in the majors.

As the San Gabriel Mountains disappeared in the fading light of day and the temperature dropped below triple digits (a balmy 99), the game settled into a classic pitchers' duel, not surprising given the fact that two of the game's best were dueling. In the bottom of the fourth, Keuchel, working with his usual quiet efficiency, got Turner on a pop-up to first, Bellinger on a ground ball to first, and Puig on a ground ball to short.

In the fifth, Kershaw threw another perfect inning: McCann hit a ground ball into the shift, third baseman Turner handled a trick bounce on a grounder from Gonzalez, and Reddick watched a 95-mile-per-hour fastball streak by for strike three.

On to the sixth, the game still tied. Keuchel became Kershaw's 10th strikeout victim and Springer number 11, flailing at a changeup that was nearly in the dirt. Bregman ground out to short to end the inning. Kershaw headed to the dugout as the first Dodger pitcher to have double-digit strikeouts in a World Series game since Hall of Famer Sandy Koufax had 10 in Game 7 of the 1965 Series.

In the bottom of the sixth, Keuchel needed one pitch to get the first out, retiring Barnes on a grounder to short. Kershaw also grounded out to short. Pitching carefully to Taylor, Keuchel walked him on five pitches, which brought up Turner.

Keuchel served up three fastballs, all low in the strike zone. When a fourth 87-mile-per-hour fastball came toward the plate higher in the zone, up toward the third baseman's messy, red beard, Turner drove it 371 feet into the left field stands for a two-out, two-run home run and a 3–1 Dodgers lead. Dodgers fans, often more laid-back than most, were on their feet and loud.

"I didn't know if it was going to be a home run or not," Turner said after the game. "I knew I backspun it pretty good. I knew I hit it really high. And I knew it was about 98 degrees. So when it's that hot here, the ball does travel a lot better....If it's 10 degrees cooler, that's probably a routine fly to left field."

"That one was a tough one to swallow," Keuchel said afterward.

Suddenly the Dodgers could breathe easier, knowing that a two-run lead with Kershaw on the mound and a superb bullpen to finish up was often more than enough. Keuchel ended the sixth by striking out Bellinger, but as *Houston Chronicle* columnist Brian T. Smith wrote afterward, "You knew that it was basically over."

With their heroes down two, anxious Astros fans were happy to see Altuve lead off the seventh. The American League batting champ came through with a ground-ball single to left. It was now or never for the Core Four—Springer, Altuve, Correa, and Bregman—to break out, as they had so many times during the regular season.

Alas, not this time. Correa ground into a force-out that erased Altuve at second. Correa was forced out at second on a Gurriel ground ball, and Brian McCann flied out to center field for the third out. The innings were dwindling down.

Kershaw, who needed just 83 pitches to make it through seven innings, was done for the night. He gave up three hits, one earned run, and recorded 11 strikeouts, his only mistake Bregman's solo home run. He became the first pitcher all season to strike out 11 Astros in a start.

In the top of the eighth, the Dodgers turned to their bullpen, a reliable bunch of arms all year for Manager Roberts. The Astros sent up three hitters, and Dodger relievers sent them all back to the dugout. In the bottom of the inning, Astros relievers got the same results.

"The Astros won Game 4 of the American League division series in Boston, but since then they lost three road games at Yankee Stadium and are three outs from losing here at Dodger Stadium," reporter David Waldstein noted on the *New York Times* blog between innings. "Obviously, they can't win the World Series if they don't win at least one game on the road."

With the Dodgers three outs away from victory, Kenley Jansen, the most effective closer in the National League, came on for the ninth. He got things started by catching Springer looking at a 92-mile-per-hour cutter in the upper part of the strike zone for strike three. The Astros slugger tossed his unused bat in frustration.

Bregman, who got Houston's only run with his solo homer, flied out to center. Jansen closed things out by retiring Altuve on a fly ball to right.

It was over. The team that had never won a World Series game still was winless. They played it close but it wasn't enough. They faced a nagging statistic: historically, the team that wins Game 1 of a best-of-seven, postseason series at home has gone on to win the series 67.3 percent of the time.

And while Keuchel pitched well, the Astros' bats were anemic. Springer struck out four times and looked bad doing it. The Astros Core Four went for a combined 2 of 15. As for everyone else in the lineup, they accounted for a single hit.

Of course, the Dodgers' Kid K had something to do with that. Kershaw finished as the first pitcher in World Series history to get 10 or more strikeouts while allowing no walks and three or fewer hits. His 78 game score, a comprehensive measure of the quality of a pitcher's start, was close to one of the greatest World Series starts ever.

Afterward, Manager Hinch was matter-of-fact about the game. "They had two big swings, we had one," he told reporters. "They had a walk right before one of their big swings, and it's 3–1. It's no more complicated than that."

CHAPTER 2

Team for Sale, Needs Work

We'll spend money, but we won't spend money we don't have.

JIM CRANE IN AN INTERVIEW WITH *PAPERCITY MAGAZINE*

In January 2018, I was sitting with Jim Crane in the boardroom near his fifth-floor office in the venerable Union Station building, the Astros headquarters. Now on the National Register of Historic Places, the red-brick building was constructed in 1911 as a terminal for the 17 rail lines that converged on Houston in the early years of the 20th century. The building now houses the club's offices and abuts Minute Maid Park.

I was talking to Crane, but it was hard to ignore the dramatic view from the boardroom windows—the banks of forest-green seats, row after row of them; the emerald-green grass of the outfield; the geometrically precise lines of the dirt base paths and pitcher's mound; the precise infield. Center field resembled a pool-table green and flawless pasture, one that looked large enough for a herd of Texas longhorns. Its spaciousness made me respect all the more the young World Series MVP who cowboys that pasture for the Astros.

In shallow right field on a gray winter morning, a dark-haired young man in shorts and a T-shirt was playing long-distance catch with a fellow in bright-orange baseball pants. He was a right-hander, throwing from a stretch each time, but from the office-building distance, I couldn't recognize him.

The Astros owner, 63, wore a white dress shirt and dark slacks, no tie. On the walls were a framed replica of his navy-blue Mules jersey from his baseball-playing days at Central Missouri State University (now the University of Central Missouri), photos of him playing golf with President Obama and Tiger Woods and a copy of a 2015 typewritten letter from former President George H. W. Bush, a longtime Houstonian who with his wife, Barbara, has box seats near home plate. ["We hate that we didn't stay long (it's an age thing, Jim), but we loved every minute and are still talking about the electricity that filled the park. It was incredible."]

Although Crane owns spectacular properties around the country—including a Pebble Beach mansion he sold for $12.5 million shortly before the Astros won the World Series—and is a millionaire many times over, he would never be described as flashy or larger-than-life. In his younger years, friends watched him vault parking meters on the streets of New Orleans while on a boozy weekend trip, but that was out of character.

A former wife described him as shy and then corrected herself. "Let's call him reserved," she said. In the stands at Minute Maid or at Potente—his upscale Italian restaurant near the ballpark—the medium-sized guy with regular features and wavy light-brown hair brushed back from a high forehead does not stand out in a crowd.

A business associate drew a contrast between Crane and sports wheeler-dealer Jerry Jones, Dallas Cowboys owner. "He [Jones] wants to be not only the man but for everybody to know he's the man," the associate told me. "Crane doesn't have that need. He doesn't have to be The Guy. Jim's not the guy who wants to be on the billboard."

Jones was a college football player and Crane a baseball player, a good one. According to the associate, that experience has made Crane a better baseball team owner than he would have been.

He's proud of his youthful diamond prowess. The legendary founder of the Astros, Judge Roy Hofheinz, used to say that as a kid he always wanted to be a ballplayer, but he had three handicaps: "I couldn't run, hit, or throw." That's not Crane, who first picked up a bat and glove at age six and played baseball and basketball well.

Crane no longer plays baseball, but he's a superb amateur golfer, a sport he first took up while caddying as a kid. At his exclusive Floridian National Golf Club in Palm City, Florida, in 2013, he played 18 holes in a foursome that included Obama. The four players split into pairs, Crane partnering with then-U.S. Trade Representative and former Dallas Mayor Ron Kirk.

In the clubhouse afterward, Obama ran into Crane's then-wife, Franci Neely Crane. "We beat your husband," the president told her, a big grin on his face. Obama's partner walked up about that time. "*We* beat your husband," Tiger Woods said, pointing at himself.

However reserved Crane is on the outside, there's an inner drive for perfection that's almost obsessive. He's relentless, never satisfied, and every detail is important. He's been known to say that he has a key to every closet in the Union Station building and has looked inside every one of them. Talking to him, you get the feeling that he'll always have something to prove to somebody.

Like a king surveying his kingdom, he was happy in the wake of the Astros' World Series triumph—as happy as a man who's never satisfied can be. When I first interviewed him almost seven years earlier, happy is not the word I would have used to describe him. On that spring morning in 2011, he was the *aspiring* owner of the 56-year-old Astros franchise, and he seemed worried that's all he might ever be. Aspiring.

A pitcher in college and a thwarted major leaguer who became a wildly successful businessman, Crane had wanted to own a major league ball club for years. If he couldn't play, he at least wanted to be around the game, and the sale of his transportation company in 2007 gave him, potentially, his owner fee.

He was already 0-for-3 when he made the Astros offer in 2011, having tried to buy the Astros in 2008 and the Chicago Cubs and the Texas Rangers in 2009. His partner in the abortive Rangers deal was Mark Cuban, although the outspoken billionaire businessman and Dallas Mavericks owner was a minority partner. Crane believes in control, as in controlling interest.

The Houston businessman, founder of the immensely successful Crane Worldwide Logistics, wasn't all that interested in talking to a politics reporter from the local newspaper—that would be me and the *Houston Chronicle*—although he was eager to refute rumors about his personal life that he worried might kill the deal he wanted so badly. The exclusive interview he granted was an effort, it seemed, to get Major League Baseball to quit stalling—as he saw it—and approve his offer to buy the team from longtime Astros owner Drayton McLane. The billionaire businessman from a small town in Central Texas, for 18 years chairman and chief executive of the club, had called a press conference weeks earlier to announce the sale to Crane, for a reported $680 million.

As I sat across from the would-be owner in the film festival office of Franci Neely Crane, he complained that Commissioner Bud Selig and MLB had turned a business deal into something personal, and he didn't like it. He grimly recounted a divorce and child-custody dispute more than a decade old that perhaps was holding up the sale. On hand that morning were his grown children to corroborate the story that he wanted to tell.

"We've worked very hard to own a team," he told me. "We think we've put a very good proposal in place and a very good set of owners, and we'll do a very good job with the team, given the chance. And we want to do what's best for baseball."

The sale of sports franchises is often a long, complicated process, since the prospective buyer must win the approval of at least two-thirds of the 30 owners and, of course, the commissioner, who has final say. The Astros' sale was expected to be relatively easy, although it had not turned out that way. At the time, Crane suspected that Major League Baseball was stalling to pressure him into agreeing to move the Astros from the National League to the American League.

Major League Baseball wanted the switch so that both leagues would have 15 teams and three 5-team divisions. A budding in-state rivalry between the Astros and the Texas Rangers would be an added bonus. Crane told me he would consider a move, but that a move was more complicated than simply saying yes.

"We signed an agreement in May, and that agreement hinges off all the economics that were presented to us," he told me. "We're paying a very handsome sum for the team, and that was based off the deal that was presented to us. That was a signed contract, and we will honor that contract. If that changes, we've told baseball that if they want us to move to the American League we'd certainly consider that, but we have to understand all the ramifications of that. That includes travel. That includes paying for a designated hitter that we don't have to pay for. That includes our TV contract."

At the same time as the potential league jump was under discussion, baseball also investigated legal issues that grew out of Crane's 1991 divorce from his first wife, Theresa Crane, who had retained custody of the two children until 2000, when Crane successfully sued for full custody. Personal issues matter to the MLB, since Commissioner Selig and the owners were still recovering from a long-running nightmare prompted by the *War of the Roses* divorce of Dodgers' owner Frank McCourt and his wife Jamie. (Whether they owned the team 50-50 was part of the family feud.)

In what may have been the most expensive divorce in American history, court documents revealed that the McCourts had been diverting revenue from the Dodgers—MLB claimed that $189 million had been "looted"—to support their, shall we say, extravagant lifestyles. McCourt needed a personal loan from Fox Broadcasting to make the Dodgers' payroll; MLB tried to take over the team.

The Cranes' divorce was nowhere near as Hollywood-spectacular as the McCourts', although the custody case did turn bitter. The *Houston Press* reported in 2000 that police were called one night to Jim Crane's residence in an exclusive neighborhood near Rice University, over what Crane's son Jared described in his 2011 interview with me as "basically an argument" that, according to his sister Krystal in the same interview, their mother "just blew out of proportion."

The other issues holding up the sale—both resolved, Crane insisted during our 2011 interview—involved business dealings. In 1997, employees of Crane's Eagle USA Airfreight filed complaints with the Equal Employment Opportunity Commission alleging discrimination against African Americans and women of childbearing age. In 2005, Eagle settled the case for about $900,000. Crane said there was no merit to the claims. "I didn't want to pay the claims, but when it costs $3 million to try them and $900,000 to pay them out, it's a business decision at that point." Crane insisted that MLB had thoroughly investigated the matter. "I was never personally accused of discriminating against anyone, and I have never discriminated with anyone," he said.

The second matter involved a Justice Department charge of war profiteering against Crane's Eagle Global Logistics. In August 2006, Eagle paid $4 million to settle a civil lawsuit alleging that the company had inflated the costs of military shipments to Iraq. The company had allegedly added 50 cents for each kilogram of freight transported to Baghdad on shipments from Dubai in 2003 and 2004. In a 2018 interview, Crane called these isolated incidents that involved two individuals in one of the company's 400 offices in 100 countries worldwide. "There was not one executive in the corporate office that knew anything about this," he said. "Once these things were validated, the company sat down with the Justice Department, paid a fine—a big fine—and we terminated the two individuals."

In the end, the MLB found nothing in these legal matters to

hold up the sale. Once Crane agreed to move the team to the American League, MLB approved the sale of the Astros within a few weeks. Years later, however, Crane was still complaining about how then-Commissioner Selig and the owners treated him.

———————————

Born in 1954 in St. Louis, Crane grew up in a suburb called Dellwood. His father was a life insurance salesman, his mother a grocery store clerk. "My dad had a great personality," Crane told the *St. Louis Post-Dispatch*. "People liked to be around him. He was kind of the life of the party. He dressed pretty neat, too" (as does Crane).

Like Hofheinz, Bob and Joyce Crane's teenage son always had a summer job, first as a caddy and then as an attendant at a parking lot outside Busch Stadium. Both jobs were ideal for a young Cardinals fan. He got to see his heroes up close and still remembers the summer he was 13 and caddying at Norwood Hills Country Club for Cardinal heroes Stan "The Man" Musial, Ken Boyer, and Dick Groat. He remembers seeing then-future Hall of Famer Lou Brock driving though his Dellwood neighborhood in a brand-new '66 Mustang.

At Central Missouri State in Warrensburg, he was an honorable mention Division II All-American as a pitcher, compiling a record of 21–8 for the Mules, with a 2.42 ERA. He still holds an NCAA record for strikeouts in a game (18), during the opening game of the Division II College World Series in 1974.

He had offers to sign professionally, including a $50,000 signing bonus, but his mother persuaded him to stay in school. An injury to his pitching shoulder during his senior year meant he would never take the mound for his beloved Cards or for any other major league team.

The injury was relatively minor and could be easily fixed now, and probably then, but Crane has no regrets that he listened to his mom.

Crane's father died of a heart attack at age 48 between his son's freshman and sophomore years in college, and he considered dropping out to work at a warehouse for $8.50 an hour. His mother called his baseball coach, Robert Tompkins, who drove to Dellwood to persuade his ace right-hander to return to Warrensburg with him.

As in high school, Crane usually worked summer jobs to supplement his scholarship money, instead of honing his skills—and attracting scouts' attention—in a summer baseball league. He considers hard work a point of pride.

"My dad was a hard worker," he told the *Post-Dispatch*. "We weren't rich, but we didn't do without anything. If you wanted something, he told me you have to work hard for it. You see a lot of that in St. Louis. A lot of the guys I grew up with and hang around with, they're hard workers.

"They're not wealthy individuals, but they're rich at heart. I think that comes from their background and where they went to school and the neighborhoods. They stay close with the people they were around and grew up with."

Crane has been a Houstonian for decades, but he still feels connected to St. Louis. He had a childhood or college friend at each of the Astros' postseason games, from Game 1 of the American League Division Series against the Red Sox, through the

Championship Series against the Yankees, and all the way through Game 7 of the World Series against the Dodgers.

The *Post-Dispatch* reported that he usually could be found with a white sheet of paper in his coat pocket with the names of friends who would attend games. He has had the same best friend since he was seven years old in Dellwood and speaks to him at least once a week.

St. Louis, he said, is "where my roots are. I grew up there, have fond memories there, and played baseball in high school and still have a lot of friends there and I always liked [the Cardinals]. I followed the team when I was a kid. I still follow the team."

After graduating from college in 1976 with a degree in industrial safety, Crane worked in Kansas City for an insurance company analyzing fire and safety risks. At age 30, he loaded up a small U-Haul trailer with all he owned and drove south to Houston at the suggestion of a former college teammate. He went to work for the friend selling airfreight and for a while worked a second job delivering freight at night.

"I'd come home from my first job, eat dinner and go back out at 8 or 9 'til midnight," he told the *Post-Dispatch*. "I always made sure I had enough money to make it work."

When he changed jobs for an extra $10,000 in salary and his new employer couldn't make payroll, he quit. He decided that he knew enough about the freight business to start his own company, so in 1984, he borrowed $10,000 from his sister and founded Eagle USA Airfreight. Starting out with one employee, Crane himself, the company grew to more than 10,000 employees with more than 400 offices in 139 countries.

When he sold Eagle USA Airfreight in 2007, he created a new

business, Crane Worldwide Logistics, providing logistics and cus-
tomized air, ocean, and ground transportation for organizations
such as Harley-Davidson, Dell, Google, and the U.S. military that
need to get their products or equipment to distant destinations
fast. A company, for example, that needs to get 10,000 pounds of
equipment to Hong Kong overnight would likely consider Crane
Worldwide Logistics.

He also acquired an energy service provider, is president and
CEO of Crane Capital Group, Inc., and owns multiple properties in
Florida, Southern California, and downtown Houston, including
two Italian restaurants near Minute Maid.

Once allowed into the august presence of MLB owners, Crane
could see firsthand that his multimillion-dollar purchase had
almost as much room for improvement as his first freight company. "The Lastros"—as my sardonic journalist friend Julie Mason
called them—had finished with a losing record in three of the
four seasons before Crane pulled out his checkbook. The year
before, the team had posted the worst record in the history of the
franchise—56 wins, 106 losses, and 40 games out of first place.

The team he bought (with nine partners) was the baseball
equivalent of an "everything must go" Sears store marooned in a
desolate shopping mall. McLane had sold off his best players, and,
to make matters worse, he had allowed the farm system to wither.
It was considered the worst in baseball.

"The fire sale left the team with players so young and inexpe-
rienced they were in danger of getting carded when they walked
into a bar," *Texas Monthly*'s Paul Burka noted.

To make matters even worse, players on the field could glance
up almost every night into a vast expanse of forest-green seats.

With the stadium's retractable roof closed, the paltry cheers from few but faithful fans were met with echoes, as if uttered in a half-empty warehouse before shipper Crane filled it up.

Businessman Crane knew about starting from scratch and building, and that's what he would have to do with the Astros. Meanwhile, he still had his other businesses to run, and there were clues in those endeavors that suggested how he would run the Astros. He is a shrewd businessman, first and foremost; the bottom line is the ultimate metric. He would run the Astros as a business, as well.

"We'll spend money," he told Chris Baldwin of *PaperCity Magazine,* "but we won't spend money we don't have."

He shared a story with Baldwin about how, when he graduated from college, his mother handed him a greeting card—with a bill inside for $220.85. Keep in mind that the young man had gone through four years at the University of Central Missouri on a baseball scholarship and had worked odd jobs during summers.

He told Baldwin: "I go, 'What are you talking about?' Mom's like, 'Well, that's what I gave you in extra money—while you were in school. By the way, it's at 4 percent interest.' Which was her house-note interest. I had to pay her back! That taught me the value of the dollar. You tell that to one of my kids, they'd think I was crazy."

The story reminded me of the motto that the Astros gave themselves at the start of the 2017 season: "Earn It." The business tycoon who owned the team no doubt approved.

One afternoon in the summer of 2013, two years after Crane took over, I played hooky from work and walked over from my *Houston*

Chronicle office to Minute Maid for a day game. The Astros were taking on the Oakland A's. I bought my general-admission ticket and found a seat—I had several thousand choices—high above left field. The players were tiny on the expanse of green below. Small knots of fans were scattered throughout the park like castaways on a desert island, less than 10,000 total in a 43,000-seat park.

We hardy few were on hand to watch the Lastros continue their long, dreary slog toward yet another season of 100-plus losses. The tinny blast of rap music or country that greeted each Astros hitter—I mean batter—echoed around the park. If I remember correctly, that was the year the hapless, dispirited team got a 0.0 Nielsen rating on Houston television.

What I didn't realize as I enjoyed my Nolan Ryan hotdog and St. Arnold's brew that afternoon—not to mention more than ample space to spread out—was that Crane and his staff had been using advanced analytics and data that were much more sophisticated than any other team in baseball. I didn't know it at the time, but the system was beginning to get results.

On June 30, 2014, nearly a year after the day game I witnessed, *Sports Illustrated* offered up what *Washington Post* columnist Thomas Boswell called "one of the most prescient cover stories in its history, proclaiming the Astros as MLB's champions of 2017." On the cover was the magnificent George Springer, the young man who would be named the 2017 Willie Mays World Series MVP.

The *Sports Illustrated* cover story about the lowly Astros' future success, written by Ben Reiter, included the subhead, "An Unprecedented Look at How a Franchise Is Going Beyond Moneyball to Build the Game's Next Big Thing...Your 2017 World Series Champs."

Allowed deep access into the Astros' front office, Reiter learned how a team of coaches, scouts, and statistics gurus were working to turn the franchise around. Crane's guys often compared the process to playing blackjack, a game where each card that's revealed offers up a certain percentage of available outcomes. A mathematically correct play for the gambler to make depends on the situation, and sometimes the correct decision doesn't feel right, even though the gambler feels obligated to make it.

It's only natural that real "astros"—NASA astronauts, that is—were cheering on the team from Space City as the three Americans went about their business inside the cozy confines of the International Space Station. Natural not only because the Astros are their hometown team—NASA's Johnson Space Center is a few miles down Interstate 45 from Minute Maid Park—but also because the thoroughly modern Astros have been constructed using NASA-inspired analytics. The team's data-driven system takes the so-called moneyball approach to a space-station level of sophistication.

"There are other teams who dabble in analytics work with data packages and video and a basic understanding of what it means, but they haven't built a robust internal team that can think about what it means to win in Houston as an Astro," said Vernon O'Donnell, an executive with STATS, the official data provider for MLB. O'Donnell told *TechRepublic* not long after the World Series triumph that his operation had lost six employees to the Astros in recent years.

The Astros' new owner bought into the system immediately and was willing to endure humiliating seasons in the baseball wilderness with the hope, shared by few initially, that success comes to those who wait. And plan. And build.

Mathematician Sig Mejdal was the intellectual powerhouse of the team's analytics. Before he transformed his passion for baseball into a profession, he had been a blackjack dealer at Lake Tahoe and a NASA researcher. When Astros General Manager Jeff Luhnow was the St. Louis Cardinals GM, he recruited Mejdal to set up a high-powered analytics department for the Cards. Mejdal followed Luhnow to Houston as director of decision sciences for the club.

Other teams were taking the analytics approach, as well, but the Astros were much more committed than most. Now with nine members toiling in the Nerd Cave, they analyze absolutely everything about players, on the field and off.

Houston, meanwhile, waited to find out whether Crane had the patience and was willing to spend the money to make it work.

"The first year our hands were tied," the Astros owner recalled years later, a few weeks after his team had reached the pinnacle. "The next two years, you start rewinding what you have. And then you start stocking the system."

CHAPTER 3

Joy in La-La Land

SERIES TIED, 1–1

Wasn't that the best game ever?

ASTROS THIRD BASEMAN ALEX BREGMAN

L ate on the night of Tuesday, October 25, 2017, George Springer was distraught. Not only had his Astros lost the first game of the World Series to Clayton Kershaw and the Dodgers the previous evening, but the budding superstar had been atrocious at the plate. The man who hit 34 homers during the regular season struck out four times, flailing at pitches like a kid befuddled by a Wiffle ball, pitches that often missed the strike zone. And his disastrous debut in Tinsel Town followed hard on a dismal 3-for-26 performance in the seven-game American League Championship Series against the New York Yankees. The Astros indispensable leadoff man, the man who gets his teammates going, was going nowhere.

There was a chance, he knew, that Manager A. J. Hinch would move him farther down in the lineup. And Springer couldn't blame him.

Hinch, a psychology major at Stanford, is a new breed of

manager. He can be firm, but John J. McGraw or Casey Stengel he's not. Not much older than his players, he talks about supporting them, building them up. And he had no such intention of shoving his star deeper into the batting order. He made that clear shortly after the game.

"He'll be leading off," he told reporters. "He had a tough night at work, and a lot of our guys did. George has struggled. But if he hits the first pitch tomorrow into the gap…you'd be amazed how good he feels."

Hinch also knew that as George Chelston Springer III goes, so go the Astros. If he's on, so are they.

Drafted in the first round in 2011, Springer was expected from the beginning to be a key component in a completely rebuilt franchise. He made his Astros debut on April 16, 2014, going 1-for-5 with a walk against the Kansas City Royals. Just hours before, he had gone 3-for-4 with a grand slam and four runs for Class AAA Oklahoma City.

His mother a former gymnast from Puerto Rico, his father a Panamanian of African descent, the Astros outfielder typified the rich diversity that characterizes the nation's fourth-largest city. Fans loved the guy, not only because he played with such panache, but also because they knew the story of his lifelong struggle with stuttering.

"It was a very isolating feeling," Springer told Tom Verducci of *Sports Illustrated*. "It makes you go into a shell and avoid being in public places and avoid speaking in public. It was tough."

Many fans knew that through sheer willpower and determination—the same qualities that made him a superb baseball player—the young man from Connecticut overcame his stuttering.

Many knew of his affiliation with Camp Say, a two-week gathering every year for young people who stutter and for their family and friends.

During the 2017 All-Star Game, he wore a microphone while playing left field and talked to Fox Sports broadcasters. The orator Demosthenes would be reluctant to do that—if the ancient Greeks played baseball—but it didn't deter Springer. He wanted people to understand that stutterers didn't have to shy away from the spotlight.

"I can't spread a message to kids and adults if I'm not willing to put myself out there," Springer explained. "I understand I'm going to stutter. I don't care. It is what it is. It's not going to stop me from talking or having fun."

He did both as the "founder" of Club Astros during the 2015 season. The young mohawk-haired outfielder anointed himself club-house DJ for the team. Before each game, he laid on the recorded music full blast and cut outlandish dance moves to the pounding, infectious beat while a fog machine wafted smoke throughout the clubhouse. His repertoire for the seventh game of the World Series would be old-school, late '70s disco funk, the music he heard his dad play on 8-track tapes while they were driving.

"He brings a lot of energy. He brings a lot of passion," Hinch said. "He's sort of the life of the party literally with what we had going on, pre- and postgame. So there's a lot of charisma that comes with George and intangibles that don't show up on a stat sheet or in a box score."

Hinch didn't go into detail about Springer's boogie nights in the clubhouse, but Carlos Correa did. "It's fog-machine time!" he explained on an Astros blog. "We'll hit the button on that thing and turn on these club lights we got, and then all of a sudden you look around and see the pitchers are all dancing, and the position players are going nuts. It gets loud in there. It's mostly hip-hop, and Latin music, and reggaeton, but we throw some country in there, too. I'm always requesting Kendrick Lamar, but there's lots of Migos and Daddy Yankee and Ozuna. It's a good mix."

Springer's inspired silliness was a reminder that he and a number of his teammates were still kids playing a kid's game—for very high stakes. (Anyone who doubts their youthful exuberance should see the post–World Series Instagram photo of José Altuve with his buds, Correa and Springer, on a kiddie ride at Walt Disney's Magic Kingdom.)

Another Springer routine, one most fans don't really notice, is also telling. When he goes to home plate to lead off, he taps the umpire on the back as he walks to the right-hand batter's box and exchanges a friendly greeting. Then he taps the catcher and greets him. Then he turns to the opposing team's dugout and tips his batting helmet to the manager and players.

"It's a nightly ritual now," former Astros broadcaster Bill Brown noted, "but if you don't attend games you might not know about it. The telecast of the games usually doesn't show it, because after the commercial break the lineups and starting pitcher are featured while Springer is getting set for his opening at bat."

When it came to Springer's hitting slump, Hinch the psychologist turned out to be Hinch the psychic. The young outfielder not only started hitting balls into the gap, he began hitting them over fences. And once he recovered his stroke, there was no stopping the Astros—in an incredible Game 2 and beyond.

Game 2 had sportswriters straining for superlatives, if not hyperbole. An instant classic. Most exciting World Series game ever played. The craziest. Beyond weird.

The melee in LA featured rallies and lead changes, power pitching, great plays in the field, and a World Series–record eight home runs, four by each team. The game's five extra-inning homers were the most in MLB history, regular season or postseason. Also, an inebriated fan tumbled into the Astros bullpen—on purpose.

"For the first time since 1970, the World Series has two teams that both won 100 games; for one night, they played like they'd each won 150," Tom Boswell of the *Washington Post* observed.

"If you like October baseball, if you like any kind of baseball, that's one of the most incredible games you'll ever be a part of," Hinch said afterward.

The slugfest started out as another pitching duel, with Rich Hill, a left-hander who relies on a wicked curveball, starting for the Dodgers and Justin Verlander, the former MVP and Cy Young Award winner, on the mound for the Astros. In one of the most astute acquisitions in recent baseball memory, Houston had acquired Verlander from the Detroit Tigers on August 31, and the veteran pitcher had already gone 5–0 during this brief stint for the Astros in the regular season, and 4–0 in postseason play. Despite the brevity of his tenure, his steadiness and maturity—not to mention his superb pitching—were big reasons the youthful Astros were in the World Series.

The tall right-hander, who had pitched in two World Series for the Tigers, struck out four of the first six Dodgers he faced and retired the first nine before giving up a leadoff walk to Chris

Taylor in the fourth. An inning-ending double play allowed him to face the minimum number of hitters through four.

The Astros had gotten to Hill in the third inning when Josh Reddick led off with a single, and Verlander bunted him over to second. A single by Springer sent him to third. With runners at the corners, Alex Bregman hit a ball to center that a diving Taylor could not quite reach and Reddick scored easily.

Hill got a second out by catching Altuve looking at a fastball for strike three, and then struck out Correa on three pitches. Despite the two strikeouts, the Astros offense was showing signs of life.

That 1–0 lead held up until the fifth when, with two outs, Joc Pederson spoiled Verlander's no-hit bid by connecting with a hanging slider and sending it over the right-center field wall.

Hill threw only 60 pitches and was visibly unhappy when manager Dave Roberts walked out to the mound and handed the ball to the first of his vaunted relief cadre. The Dodgers starter had allowed only one run on three singles and a walk and struck out seven, but all season Roberts had tried to avoid having his pitchers go through the same lineup three times unless they had to. The analytics guys had taught him that familiarity breeds hitters' contempt.

The manager's adherence to the numbers was a reminder that the Dodgers were as devoted to analytics as the Astros; their department just wasn't as well known. As baseball writer and blogger Keith Law pointed out, the 2017 Series featured the team with the largest analytics department—that would be the Dodgers—pitted against the team that was most aggressive in using analytics—the Astros.

Law noted that the Front Office page of the Dodgers' website listed 48 people under the label "Baseball Operations." Thirteen had "analyst" as part of their job title; another eight had "research" in their title. The crosstown Angels, he noted, listed eight executives. Period. The Astros' employ nine in their so-called Nerd Cave.

On this night, LA's analytics army had Roberts making forced marches to the mound almost as often as a basic trainee being punished for missing reveille. The Dodgers tied a World Series record for the number of pitchers, nine, to appear in a single game. The only other team to use nine pitchers was the Chicago White Sox in Game 3 of the 2005 World Series—against none other than the Houston Astros on October 25, exactly 12 years earlier.

As in the Series opener, the bottom of the sixth was the fulcrum. With two outs and Verlander cruising, Taylor walked and shortstop Corey Seager, who had slammed 22 homers during the regular season, came to the plate. Verlander got ahead in the count—one ball, two strikes—and tried to power a 97-mile-per-hour fastball by the young shortstop for the third out. Seager screamed like a Taylor Swift concertgoer as he heard the crack of the bat and saw the ball sailing over the left field fence. Dodgers 3, Astros 1.

Hinch went to his bullpen after pinch hitting for Verlander in the top of the seventh. Relievers Will Harris, Joe Musgrove, and Ken Giles held the Dodgers scoreless in the bottom of the seventh. "Then," Jake Kaplan of the *Houston Chronicle* wrote, "madness ensued."

After Bregman started the eighth with a ground-rule double off Brandon Morrow, Roberts called on closer Kenley Jansen, the Dodger's 265-pound intimidator who notched 41 of 42 saves during the regular season. Jansen got Altuve to ground out, but Bregman advanced to third and then scored on a single by Correa. The Dodgers bullpen had not surrendered a run through 28 consecutive innings of the postseason. Gurriel popped out and McCann struck out to end the inning. Dodgers 3, Astros 2.

In the regular season, the Dodgers had been an incredible 98–0 when they carried a lead into the ninth. But this wasn't the regular season.

Tension mounted in laid-back LA, as Jansen walked to the mound in the top of the ninth. The burly, hard-throwing right-hander has 12 saves in 12 opportunities in the postseason, a record for a reliever at the start of his career. He was three outs away from his second six-out save of the season, ready to send the Astros home to Houston in a slippery two-games-to-none hole.

Marwin Gonzalez stepped to the plate. He had been Mr. Dependable all year, at bat and in the field—he can play several positions—but he was hitting a pathetic .150 in his last 12 games. Down 0–2 in the count, the Astros left fielder slammed a solo home run to tie the game. The last time Jansen had given up a home run after running the count to 0–2 had been 82 hitters ago. As Gonzalez rounded the bases, Dodger Stadium was silent. In shock.

Jon Tayler of *Sports Illustrated* was impressed with what Gonzalez had done, given how unlikely it was. "Jansen had faced 258 batters in the regular season and given up only five homers, and none since Sept. 22," Tayler noted. "Opposing hitters had posted a mere .189 batting average off of his cutter this year. In his career, batters have hit a microscopic .082/.088/.123 when put in an 0–2 hole."

Gonzalez himself was impressive, even though he often got

overlooked among the constellation of stars in the Astros' lineup. "He's huge," Hinch said. "If I wanted to give Altuve a day off during the season, he can play second, short for Correa, third for Bregman, first for Yuli. I could put him in center if I wanted to. It's like having multiple players in one. And not just that he can do it, he can do it well."

Verlander told Gonzalez he was going to hit a home run. "I was watching George's home run on the TV, the same spot I was watching Marwin's, as superstitious as we are," he told reporters after the game. "I told Marwin the inning before, I told him, he was going to win the ballgame for us. I didn't think it was going to be a game-tying home run, I thought it was going to be a game-winning. That's what I told him....And I was in the exact same spot as George's home run because, why not? The inning before we scored a couple of runs, I'm going to be in the same spot." (So much for analytics.)

After the home run, Jansen got Reddick to pop out to second and retired pinch hitter Carlos Beltrán on a fly ball to center. He then allowed a solid two-out double to a resurgent Springer. With the go-ahead run on base, Jansen was able to retire Bregman on a grounder to short. Springer was left stranded, but in hindsight his solid double was a portent.

Astros reliever Giles shut down the Dodgers in the bottom of the ninth. The incredible game continued.

In the 10th, the littlest Astro slapped the ball over the fence, Altuve's sixth home run of the postseason. Correa followed with a round-tripper of his own, giving the Astros a 5–3 lead. Altuve and Correa became the first teammates in World Series history to hit extra-inning home runs in the same game, not to mention doing it back-to-back. Altuve, Correa, and Springer also made the Astros the first team to hit three homers in extra innings of a postseason game.

The young shortstop punctuated his homer with an in-your-face bat flip, and, in the words of the *Chronicle*'s Kaplan, "channeled his inner Yasiel Puig when asked about it after the game."

"I don't know why my bats are so slippery," the cocky, young Correa told reporters. He flashed a mischievous grin.

It wasn't over yet. Giles walked to the mound determined to hold the lead. He couldn't. The man who pitched a perfect ninth began the 10th by surrendering a leadoff home run to the pugnacious Puig, the man who licks the pine tar off his bats with a prodigious tongue. The Astros reliever struck out two batters, but then things fell apart. LA tied things up on a walk to Logan Forsythe and a single by Kike Hernández. When Forsythe slid across home plate, normally blasé LA fans went crazy.

For the Astros, the game seemed to be spiraling out of control. Were their youth and inexperience catching up with them at a most inopportune time? Cameras picked up Verlander—at 34, the team's new old head—standing at the end of the dugout in a sweaty T-shirt and shouting to his teammates. He had popped out of the tunnel leading to the clubhouse.

What did he say?

Remembering that moment after the game, he launched into an earnest soliloquy: "It's so easy in this game to get down, especially when—I mean, we have the TV on before the games. You see everyone saying how great this Dodger bullpen is and how our offense hasn't been going. It's so easy to say, 'Man, we're probably not going to win this game, down two against one of the best bullpens in baseball.'

"I just wanted to really remind these guys how great they are. I've pitched against them, I know how good they are. It doesn't matter how good a pitcher you are, this lineup can hurt you so quickly. And I guess maybe that was just my message, stay positive. Remember how good you are. And just play the game. It's only two runs.

"This team, since I've been here, and I know it hasn't been that long, but two runs is nothing. And all of a sudden two runs seemed like it was the Grand Canyon. And I just kind of—I don't even know if anybody heard me, but I was just trying to remind these guys two runs is nothing."

Relieving Giles was Chris Devenski, a hard thrower whose eccentric delivery makes it look like he's short-arming his pitches. He almost threw the game away before making his first pitch. With the winning run at second base, he whirled and tried to pick off the runner, but his throw was off the mark. Fortunately for the Astros, the ball hit the base umpire in the leg instead of rolling toward the wall. Devenski took a deep breath and got Taylor to fly out to center to end what could have been total disaster (not just partial).

In the top of the 11th, Springer walked to the plate. The man who fanned four times the night before, the man tempted to doubt himself, saw a pitch he liked and powered a two-run home run to right-center field. It looked like the ball might bounce off the wall, but in the hot LA air it carried up and over. Leading 7–5, the Astros went berserk.

"George Springer etched his name in Astros' lore with the biggest hit in franchise history Wednesday night at Dodger Stadium," the *Chronicle*'s Kaplan wrote.

Yes, but not quite. The Dodgers still had the bottom of the inning, and the way things had gone, no one in the stadium was leaving. This was La-La Land, after all, where Andy Hardy gets the girl, the good guys vanquish the gangsters, the home team hits the winning basket as the seconds die down on the scoreboard. And where visiting pitchers deliver up hittable fastballs to angels in white.

It was Hollywood, and true to form, the lonely guy at the end of the Dodger bench, an infielder named Charlie Culberson who was playing for the Oklahoma City Dodgers of the Pacific Coast League not long ago, walked up to the plate and slapped a Devenski fastball over the fence. Fans in Dodger blue chased the blues. They leaped to their feet. They hugged each other, exchanged high fives. The noise was deafening. The upper deck of Dodger Stadium swayed.

The Dodgers were down by one. They had a chance. The ever-dangerous Puig, the man who led off the 10th with a home run, walked to the plate, determined to tie the game.

Devenski got him. Game over. 7–6. Now, reporters could write it: the amazing Astros have won their first World Series game ever.

"I've been part of some exciting games, But, no, none like this," Verlander said afterward. "Exciting, thrilling and for it to be in the World Series…this is an instant classic. To tell you the truth, I was rooting so hard I almost fainted three times. I was cheering so loud I had to stop, so I wouldn't pass out."

"Wasn't that the best game ever?" young Bregman exclaimed in the noisy clubhouse. (And it was, for a little while.)

The baseball world was in a swoon, as well. "The Houston Astros have their first World Series win in franchise history, and they had to earn it," wrote Grant Brisbee at SBNation. "They had to clamber over the narratives and self-doubt to reclaim their identity as the lumber-thumping monsters under every pitcher's bed, and they had to figure out which wire to cut, while the timer on the homemade bomb was ticking down to zero."

Hall of Famer Craig Biggio was less florid but no less awestruck. "This means so much to our city, he told *Chronicle* columnist Jenny Dial Creech. "There are still people trying to get back in their homes. For these guys to continue to play like they did in that difficult time, and for the fan base to rally around our boys is pretty amazing."

"That game was probably as nerve-wracking as it is in the stands for everybody else," an ebullient Springer told reporters. "You know, who's on the other team, you know who's on deck, and you know who's hitting. And when that last out is made, you finally breathe."

Springer laughed. "That's the craziest back-and-forth game I've ever been in," he said. "And it's only Game 2."

He's back, man," Correa said, smiling as he listened to Springer. "He gets really scary when he's back."

Springer and his fellow Astros were headed home—home where they rarely lost, home to a city that had lost much.

CHAPTER 4

Harvey Looms

*It's like putting a bowling ball down in the middle of an alley—
where will it roll?*

METEOROLOGIST ERIC BERGER ON TRYING TO PREDICT HARVEY'S PATH

Some 10 weeks before the Astros' monumental win in the second game of the 2017 World Series, Houstonians were slogging through the usual summer heat and humidity. August is typically a tropical mess of a month in southeast Texas. It shows no mercy to residents, who endure long days of highs in the upper 90s, lows around 80, heat indices surging past 100 degrees, and maybe an afternoon shower that contributes to the sultriness. (The spectrum of seasons in Houston are nearly summer, summer, and quick cold snap.) Coolish days at the start of August 2017 and some welcome rains, even a few heavy downpours, had brought some relief, but broiling temperatures and stifling humidity soon reasserted themselves.

On August 13, a Sunday, Houstonians paid little notice to the tropical wave forming off the coast of Africa more than 5,000 miles away. Weather watchers began paying more attention to it four days later when the National Hurricane Center issued an advisory about the growing storm heading toward the Caribbean. Officially designated a tropical storm, it was christened Harvey on August 17.

As a name, Harvey didn't seem all that threatening. For movie fans of a certain age (and TCM watchers), Harvey was the name of the giant imaginary rabbit that appeared in visions bedeviling Elwood P. Dowd (Jimmy Stewart) in the 1950 movie of the same name. For others, perhaps the name called to mind notable Americans of the 20th century like Harvey Haddix and Harvey Milk and Paul Harvey. (Disgraced Hollywood mogul Harvey Weinstein had not yet forced himself into the national zeitgeist.)

Harvey seemed about to blow itself out after rampaging the Caribbean; it was downgraded to a tropical wave three days later. Coastal Texans went about their business. School was starting soon, the solar eclipse was coming, and Houstonians were asking themselves almost every day at the office: "How 'bout them Astros?" Amazingly, the team that had hobbled through three consecutive 105-loss seasons was running away with the division. The coltish, young Astros were, arguably, the best team in baseball—and certainly the most fun to watch.

———————————

"Hot enough for ya?" That was the other question people always asked in August. Newcomers to Houston soon learned that the hot, humid weather was a point of perverse pride—and had been since the city's founding in the 1830s.

In one of my weekly "Native Texan" columns in the *Houston*

Chronicle, I wrote about a distinguished visitor to Houston in May 1837. John James Audubon stepped off the steamer *Yellow Stone*, clambered up the slippery bank of Buffalo Bayou—within walking distance of today's Minute Maid Park—and caught his first glimpse of the new town, capital city of the Republic of Texas.

Slogging past filthy tents, half-finished houses, and roofless buildings in a clearing hacked out of a pine forest, the world-famous naturalist made his way to the "mansion" of newly elected President Sam Houston. A gathering of cabinet members welcomed their distinguished guest into a rough 12-by-16 log cabin consisting of two rooms separated by a dog run. Audubon couldn't help but notice how cluttered and filthy everything was, in the anteroom and in the president's private chamber. While impressed with Sam Houston, he would recall that "the place of his abode can never be forgotten."

Hanging around the mud-caked, mosquito-ridden town for a few days, Audubon wandered into the roofless capitol building. When Congress assembled six days after his arrival, he noted that it had rained the night before and the floor was a lake. Lawmakers glanced down at their wet boots and soaked pant legs and at the soggy, smudged papers on their desks and promptly adjourned. They stepped out of the building into stinking streets that relied on the appetite of feral hogs for sanitation. Drinking water came from the bayou, which also was the sewer. Inside the filthy tents and rudimentary houses were Houstonians laid low by typhoid and dysentery.

Frank Lubbock, a passenger on the first steamship to reach Houston via Buffalo Bayou, recalled decades later: "It was a very muddy place…with very poor drainage, so that, with the immense wagon trade, the roads and streets, although very wide and hand-some, were almost impassable in wet weather."

One afternoon a young Texas immigrant named Granville Rose was walking with his buddies as they strolled along the bayou when they were set upon by a swarm of mosquitoes "as large as grasshop-pers." The young men splashed into the bayou to escape, only to dis-cover that the water was aboil with alligators. Their mad scramble to shore left one of their party stranded on the opposite bank, so the oth-ers found a canoe to ferry him back across. As the vessel nosed into the bank, a large panther sprang out of the brush and bounded away.

"Houston is now one of the muddiest and most disagreeable places on earth," another early-day visitor, John Winfield Scott Dancy, observed in 1838.

Why would Lubbock and Rose and an ever-growing number of immigrants have made their way to one of the muddiest and most disagreeable places on earth? Many had been wooed by Augustus Chapman Allen and his younger brother John Kirby Allen, two young real-estate promoters from New York City touting "an abun-dance of excellent spring water and enjoying the sea breeze in all its freshness," a city that's "handsome and beautifully elevated, salubrious and well-watered." Actually, the city then and now sits only about 50 feet above sea level, and is riven by a complex net-work of bayous, rivers, and lakes that feed into Galveston Bay. From the beginning, those waterways have flooded regularly.

Despite the fact that one of the Allens died at 28 of a "bilious fever"—possibly yellow fever or malaria—and that both brothers were Yankee hucksters nonpareil, people yearning to start anew kept coming.

So why would people live in this "swampy, soupy, overheated" city, as football writer Spencer Hall describes the 21st-century iteration. "It's the most animated town I have seen in Texas," an early Houstonian exclaimed. And still is.

Sixty-odd years after the Allen brothers envisioned a thriving town along the bayou, second- and third-generation Houstonians were quick to seize an opportunity, quick to build. The Monday after the great hurricane of 1900 devastated the state's leading port city, killing between 8,000 and 12,000 people, the Houston City Council had three items on its agenda: humanitarian aid for Galveston, repairing Houston's storm-damaged roofs, and expediting a plan for dredging a ship channel. If you've hacked a thriving city out of a malarial swamp, gouging out a 50-mile ditch to the sea was not all that daunting.

In addition to the 1900 hurricane that devastated their coastal neighbor—still the deadliest natural disaster in the United States—Houstonians have braced for and survived numerous major blows down through the decades. They've paved bayou channels and gouged out reservoirs, trying to cope with many Texas-sized floods during Houston's first century of existence. The floods often were the outgrowth of tropical storms or hurricanes. Longtime residents measure signature life events using those traumatic weather events as markers: *Wasn't she born right around Carla? Was it before Allison or after that we went on that trip to Colorado?* They've endured Alicia and Rita, Ike and Harvey, just in the past few years.

———————————

Harvey in its early stages, a couple of weeks beyond the dog days of August, bore watching but seemed of relatively minor consequence.

Harvey revived was another matter. The slow-moving system grew and intensified as its remnants moved over Mexico's Yucatán Peninsula and back over the warm Gulf waters. It strengthened into a tropical depression on August 23 and was plodding toward landfall somewhere along the Gulf Coast southwest of Houston.

Even the most reliable weather forecasters couldn't predict what Houston was about to undergo. At 6:34 on Tuesday morning, August 22, trusted part-time meteorologist Eric Berger of the popular website Space City Weather noted that Houstonians could be facing a "very wet weekend due to tropical moisture."

Berger was seeing a weakened Harvey that just wouldn't die. The mass of meteorological energy lingered and was reforming into a storm that could hit the south central Texas coast with heavy rainfall. Dawdling systems like Harvey are dangerous, because they yield large amounts of rainfall (although no one imagined that "large amounts" would mean 60 inches).

It was still too early for any real anxiety, but as Harvey intensified on Wednesday afternoon, forecasters—like the Astros' sophisticated analytics department—were running their own calculations. Houstonians watched and waited.

My wife, Laura, and I were in Austin, nearly 200 miles inland. We were looking forward to a reunion with far-flung adult children (England; Washington, DC, Los Angeles, Austin) who rarely get together all at once. Harvey was playing havoc with their flight schedules and plans. Laura, who had experienced a couple of Houston hurricanes—and had helped coordinate Katrina coverage as an editor for the *Houston Chronicle*—was anxious to get home. I saw no need to rush. Like many, my attitude was, *Hey, don't weathermen always exaggerate?*

As Laura quickly reminded me, my hurricane judgment was suspect. I was the "fool" who years ago drove to meet a hurricane, checking into a deserted La Quinta Motel on Galveston's seawall a few hours before Alicia made landfall during the night. ("I won't charge you," the desk clerk had told me, handing me a pillow and sheets and wishing me good luck as he hustled out the lobby door.)

"I survived," I reminded Laura. "And I got a good story out of it."

She was not amused. We drove home to Houston.

Encountering the rain as we drove eastward, it was obvious that the words hurricane, landfall, and Texas had begun to sink in. On Houston's outskirts, gas station lines stretched into the street, and supermarket parking lots filled up; within hours, the bare shelves would resemble Soviet-era commissaries. At Home Depot, customers were carting out flats of plywood for nailing over windows.

By Thursday morning, August 24, it was beginning to register with Gulf Coast residents that soaking rains and some flooding were inevitable. But where exactly would the storm strike and how hard? Those were the questions.

The various tracking models and forecasts put landfall somewhere between Brownsville to the south and Corpus Christi and Matagorda up the coast, more than 200 miles south of Houston along what Texans call the Coastal Bend. (Look at a map, and you'll see why.) Still, the city could get some heavy rainfall, maybe by Saturday. Tropical winds would not really be a problem for Houston; a stalled storm with heavy moisture could be.

Anxious coastal residents began working out a plan for themselves and their families. Should they hunker down and shelter in place or pack a few belongings, get in the car, and head inland to a motel or to relatives? During Hurricane Rita in 2005, thousands of Houston-area residents evacuated, and the clogged roads in a region of more than 6 million people became more of a danger than the storm itself. With Harvey approaching and growing stronger, Houston Mayor Sylvester Turner and his counterparts up and down the coast soon would be facing a hard decision.

"It's like putting a bowling ball down in the middle of an alley—where will it roll? Harvey is going to be something like that," Berger wrote on Thursday night, the 24th.

On Friday, Houstonians awoke to worsening news from forecasters, including Berger, a former science reporter for the *Houston Chronicle* who became a certified meteorologist. "For Texas," he wrote in his 6:15 a.m. post, "there will be two epochs of Harvey: the catastrophic effects for the Texas coast from wind and surge during the next day or so for the central Texas coast, and the unfolding, widespread, major flood event from Saturday through the middle of next week for a large swath of the state, including Houston."

As Harvey lingered in the Gulf long enough to muscle up to Charles Atlas proportions, Berger's Space City blog—which touts its "hype-free forecasts" developed a devoted following and was being shared widely across Houston-area Facebook pages. Elsewhere, officials in some coastal towns were strongly advising residents to evacuate.

A hurricane was going to punish the Texas coast—that was now certain. The winds are the issue for areas where a storm makes landfall, while inland areas are concerned about rainfall. The huge, unanswered question for Houston, the sprawling metropolis some 40 miles inland, a city creased by bayous headed to the sea like the lines on the palm of a hand, was how much rain would fall. Floods had become increasingly severe over the years, even without a hurricane. Although government officials and civic leaders had willfully ignored the problem, a city relentlessly spreading amoeba-like into the surrounding coastal plain was also paving over prairie; water had no place to drain except into bayous unable to accommodate an influx of this magnitude.

On Friday, Harvey exploded into a Category 4 hurricane. Radar images showed the monster storm expanding across much of the Gulf of Mexico. Tornados lashing out from inside the huge, gray cloud threatened coastal communities. As if on cue, rain bands, like commandos probing the shoreline prior to an invasion, made landfall.

Harvey arrived in the dark of night. The Category 4 hurricane stormed ashore Friday about 10:00 p.m. between the city of Corpus Christi, population 400,000, and the picturesque, little beach town of Rockport. Its first victim, shortly before 10:00 p.m., was a village called Tivoli (pronounced Tie-VO-li in Texas), 20 miles inland. Harvey's 130-mile-per-hour winds blew away houses, knocked down buildings, and sent rivers and creeks raging over their banks.

News reports from the area were grim. Rockport was in shambles. Beach houses on stilts were flattened. The historic commercial district was a jumble of shattered glass, bricks, and stone. Huge, historic live oaks lay on their sides or atop splintered houses.

Port Aransas, a laid-back, little community on Mustang Island—everybody's favorite beach town, *Texas Monthly* called it—was 80 percent destroyed. A popular destination for so-called Winter

Texans, people from the Midwest, usually retirees, who flee the winter cold by spending half the year in Port A, would not be returning post-Harvey. There was nothing to return to. Mobile homes and house trailers lay on their sides scattered like pieces of a child's electric train. Boats in the harbor lay half-submerged.

Houston waited, wondering where a fickle, powerful Harvey would wander. Some experts suggested that landfall would weaken the storm and that it would continue to dissipate as it moved inland. That had happened with previous hurricanes. If Harvey adhered to that pattern, the city likely would see some heavy rainfall in the coming days, not much else. Houstonians were used to a lot of water, or thought they were.

The next day, Saturday, thunderstorm bands from Harvey brought intermittent rain to the greater Houston region. Authorities began to issue flash-flood warnings as usual during rainstorms, when city streets typically become running streams and bayous become roiling torrents of muddy, debris-choked water. Still, the situation appeared manageable. Relying on its system of drainage ditches, bayous, rivers, and lakes feeding into Galveston Bay, the city was basically prepared to handle 10–15 inches of rain, although that amount would cause some localized flooding. Twenty or more inches would be a different story for a city that sits only about 50 feet above sea level.

Houstonians stuck close to home, kept an eye on the Weather Channel, and hoped that maybe their city would avoid the storm's wrath, as it had in 2005 when Hurricane Rita made landfall east of the city.

Sadly, they were wrong. Harvey was about to lay siege to the nation's fourth-largest city. The meandering storm would stall over the Houston area and unleash 34 trillion gallons of water, stun uber-confident Texans, and prompt a government and civilian rescue effort across the region that would gain worldwide admiration.

Harvey would drown the city in nearly 60 inches of rainfall, the heaviest amount ever recorded in the continental United States from one rain event. (Average *annual* rainfall in Houston is about 49 inches.) It would fill nearly 50,000 homes with fetid, disease-bearing water and displace tens of thousands of people. Damage estimates would climb to nearly $200 billion, surpassing Hurricane Katrina's toll in 2005. No one imagined.

At least 88 people died, more than 50 from the Houston area. The dead included a family of six—two grandparents and four grandchildren—who were swept into a bayou while trying to escape the floodwaters in a van, a Houston police officer on his way to work during the flood, a mother whose three-year-old daughter was found clinging to her lifeless body.

And yet, Harvey also prompted countless expressions of strength, compassion, and resilience. Houstonians and volunteers from around the nation waded through those dangerous waters. They literally carried people from their drowned-out homes to safety. They worked in shelters for hours at a time to make sure their neighbors had a hot meal, a warm, dry place to lie down at night, a safe place where they could ease their minds about their children's well-being. If not for their efforts—their boats, their high-water vehicles, their time and energy, their ingenuity, their money—the death toll might have been much higher.

The slogan the Astros adopted? Houston Strong? The rescuers and the resilient, the helpers and the caring—young and old;

men, women, and children; black, white, and brown—embodied those two words. It may be a stretch, but I would argue that without those people, the Astros might not have won a World Series. Houstonians set a standard, gave the team something to aspire to as they went about their business of playing baseball. At the same time, the crisis unfolding around the players helped keep them loose. With Houstonians losing their homes and belongings, even their lives, the Astros played with the realization that baseball wasn't the most important thing in the world. Paradoxically, they played better when they had something else to think about.

That first weekend, though, neither the Astros nor their fellow Houstonians knew what was coming. As a stormy Saturday evening became an unimaginable Sunday morning, an epic disaster was unfolding.

CHAPTER 5

Harvey Hits Houston—Hard

What is happening to my hometown?

HARRIS COUNTY SHERIFF ED GONZALEZ

Maya Wadler nervously stayed awake listening to the pounding rain early Sunday morning in the family's single-story home in Willow Meadows, a comfortable neighborhood in southwest Houston. Her mother, Freda, and her older sister Ariel were spending the night with neighbors in a two-story home nearby. Since the neighbors didn't have enough beds to accommodate the entire Wadler family, Maya, 17, and her father, Michael Wadler, a Houston attorney, stayed home.

The dark-haired, dark-eyed teenager worried while her father slept. She busied herself talking to friends on her cell phone and piling possessions atop beds, tables, countertops—any higher surface available that was off the floor. She and her family had been through this before. Their '60s-era ranch-style home had taken on a foot of water in Houston's 2015 Memorial Day flood. Although nobody was injured, the house was repaired and the family managed to spend the night at home during the downpour.

Earlier in the evening, Michael had reassured his family: hey, we survived Memorial Day; we'll survive Harvey.

By late Saturday night, it was becoming distressingly evident that this was not Memorial Day 2015. In an unprecedented move, the National Weather Service issued a dire warning early Sunday: "Flash Flood Emergency for Catastrophic Life-Threatening Flooding."

Sheets of water were invading neighborhoods across Houston, including the Wadlers' Willow Meadows. About two in the morning, streetlights and porch lights revealed water running across the yard, streaming inexorably toward the house. A couple of hours later it broke through. Maya sat cross-legged on her bed, staring at the water rising in her room "in utter shock."

Later, she remembered feeling frozen, unable to move. After a moment, she scrambled off the bed, gathered up towels in the bathroom, and tried to stuff them around door frames. "I thought I could stop the water," Maya recalled. Soon they were floating. "I was freaking!"

She was staring out a window at the running river that had been their street, when a spotlight homed in on her. It was a fire-rescue team in a boat. Once the firefighters saw her, they nosed their boat toward the house. She quickly woke her father, and their rescuers arrived at the door and told the Wadlers that they must evacuate with them—NOW! It was going to get worse, a lot worse, the firefighters warned. (The Wadlers' house would eventually sustain about four feet of water.)

Confused and scared, father and daughter sloshed through a foot of water in the house, frantically throwing on some clothes. Into a plastic garbage bag they tossed a computer, contact lenses, and a set of small black leather boxes called Tefillin, containing scrolls of parchment inscribed with verses from the Torah. Observant male Jews wear them during weekday morning prayers. They stuffed their cell phones into ziplock bags, shrugged on life jackets, and stepped into the rescue boat docked for the moment in their front yard. Michael couldn't find any shoes, so he headed off into the cold, rainy darkness barefoot, in shorts and a shirt. Maya tugged on her blue rain boots.

"We didn't appreciate how dangerous it was to be out on the water," Michael recalled weeks later. Maya remembers the surreal feeling: "We didn't even ask where this boat was taking us. We just got in."

———————

"I remember watching it rain and it wasn't stopping, and I remember thinking, 'What is happening to my hometown?'" Harris County Sheriff Ed Gonzalez recalled.

Harris County Judge Ed Emmett recalled a similar response. "You start wondering, when is this going to end?"

Sunday dawned, although there was no sign of a sun. The rain was still coming down hard when Gonzalez and four of his deputies climbed into a five-ton truck they had commandeered and headed east on the city's Loop 610. They came across a man standing atop a wall, a wall they knew was eight feet tall; the water was already above his waist. Trying to figure out how to rescue him, they flagged down a truck from Houston Metro, the city's mass transit agency, hoping the driver had a rope. He didn't have a rope, but he had a water hose. The water was rising; the hose would have to do.

"He was holding on for dear life," Gonzalez recalled, "so we were able to form a human chain and used the water hose to give him something to hang on to."

The man told the sheriff that he was a security guard, and that he had stayed at his post until two in the morning, doing his job, until he could stay no longer. He didn't know how to swim.

Gonzalez, 48, a former Houston homicide detective and City Council member, could swim. He went into the water numerous times during the next several days. "You could see the water spinning, 8 to 10 feet of dark water," he said. "If you go under, you may not surface. You say a prayer, lean on your faith and your training."

The Harris County Sheriff's Office oversees the sixth-largest jail in America, a group of buildings along Buffalo Bayou as it flows through downtown that typically houses nearly 10,000 inmates. Gonzalez knew that if those buildings flooded or if they started losing power, "we might be on the brink of collapse." Fortunately, that didn't happen. Flooding in tunnels between buildings was the only problem.

Gonzalez could see firsthand, though, that his hometown was drowning. His fellow Houstonians had to act, immediately. He and other first responders, however dedicated and heroic, couldn't do it alone. Houstonians and volunteers from miles away, including other states, created an ad hoc rescue force that resembled the Dunkirk evacuation of World War II.

Judge Emmett put out a call for boats on Sunday afternoon,

but the boats were already on their way. "People were going to put them in the water whether I put out a call or not," he said.

In their eagerness to rescue as many people as possible, first responders sometimes forgot where they deposited them, Emmett remembered with a laugh weeks later. "We had to go back and find 'em at strip centers, convenience stores, anywhere it was dry."

For a city that loves its cars and trucks and that relies on looping, soaring freeways to get around the sprawling metropolis, the scene of boats plying the streets and highways—fishing boats, fan boats, kayaks, rafts, pirogues, whatever floated—was almost too bizarre to believe. The ad hoc flotilla resembled a nautical promenade on the Grand Canal in Venice. Except for the gas station signs and the telephone poles barely topping the water. Except for the submerged cars and trucks. And except for the tired, cold, and anxious men, women, and children, often with bedraggled pets in their arms, who were passengers on those boats, headed under gray, drizzly skies toward some kind of shelter.

"The government can only do so much for a city of 7 million people," Houston writer John Nova Lomax told the *Washington Post*. "We have a lot of outdoorsy people down here and a lot of people with boats and lifted trucks and there's a Texas machismo here that says, 'I'm not going to wait, I'm going to get out there and help people myself!'"

A convoy of rescuers driving in along Interstate 10 from the east caught the public's fancy. Calling themselves the Cajun Navy, they were sport fishermen and duck hunters from Louisiana, good ol' boys as adept at using social media as they were at luring ducks into shooting range with their hand-carved duck calls. They had brought their high-clearance pickup trucks, bass boats, airboats, skiffs, and pirogues to help rescue people in Houston, Beaumont, Port Arthur, and points in-between.

They were well aware that during Katrina, hundreds of Texans heading in the opposite direction had crossed the border to help with rescue efforts. Both Texans and Louisianans were residents of the so-called Cajun Corridor, connected not only by ethnic ties but also by fishing and oil-refinery jobs in both states. The Cajun Navy was repaying the favor.

"I vividly remember that many Texans came to Louisiana's aid, which was incredible to me," Taylor Aucoin of Baton Rouge told reporters. She and her husband were aided by the Zello app that allowed them to radio in rescue requests to volunteers on the ground in flooded areas.

"I can't really describe the heartbreak that I feel now for Texans," she said. "It's a very small thing we can do from here to kind of repay the favor for the help we received last year and countless other times."

Volunteers were welcome, as even Houston's public officials found themselves under water. Harris County Commissioner Rodney Ellis was asleep at home Saturday night when wife Licia woke him to say the roof was leaking. They put a trash can under the leak and went back to sleep. At 3:00 a.m. Sunday, Licia's phone rang. It was Mayor Sylvester Turner; he had tried to call her husband, but the commissioner's phone was on vibrate mode.

"Do you have any boats?" the mayor asked. Ellis, half asleep, thought his longtime political ally—they had served together in the Texas Legislature—said votes.

"No! Boats!" the mayor shouted. "Boats!"

The commissioner didn't have boats, but he did have dump trucks in his precinct. He got in touch with county employees, who drove through the storm to the main office, gassed up the big, heavy vehicles, and headed into the dark, flooded neighborhoods. Their headlights became beacons of hope for people waiting to be rescued.

People like the Wadlers.

The rescue boat took them and two others to a highway feeder road where they precariously climbed into a waiting dump truck with about 20 other flood victims. They took a circuitous route to a fire station on South Main. A gray and desolate dawn revealed a Houston with flooded vehicles, homes nearly submerged, with only a roof visible, people waiting to be rescued.

"It's just an apocalyptic lake," Michael Wadler remembered thinking.

At the fire station, firefighters found them dry clothes and served them breakfast. "They were ridiculously kind to us," Wadler recalled. "You just don't realize how vulnerable you are."

Later, Freda Wadler found her husband a pair of shoes donated to a shelter set up at the George R. Brown Convention Center near Minute Maid Park. They managed to score a hotel room that night for the whole family.

"I can't express how grateful I am," Ariel Wadler later wrote on Facebook. "Everything I have lost can be replaced, it is just stuff. Through tragedy comes something wonderful. I cannot express how grateful I am to have such great family and friends. I live in an amazing community."

Like the Wadlers, like many Houstonians, Bill White knew floods firsthand. In the upscale Memorial neighborhood of west Houston, on a bend of Buffalo Bayou where willows normally bow gently over placid water, he was trying to get some work done on Sunday morning. The roar of incessant rain—like a runaway train, he recalled—was making it hard to concentrate.

The 63-year-old businessman was home alone; wife Andrea, a *Houston Chronicle* editorial writer and author of young-adult books, was out of town. He had played tennis on Saturday morning, indoors.

"I was checking my email and writing a long piece analyzing how index funds and ETFS were changing the market," he recalled weeks later.

Twelve years earlier, White had been Houston's mayor and had won nationwide acclaim for welcoming more than 200,000 Katrina evacuees from New Orleans, many of whom stayed in Houston and started new lives for themselves. On this Sunday morning in August, he was about to become an evacuee himself.

"I used to follow weather closely; it was part of my job," White said. "But remembering the briefings I used to get in our worst-case-scenario planning, more than 30 inches of rain seemed almost implausible."

As the rain continued its pounding and the water breached the bayou behind the backyard, White put his work aside and began preparing for the inevitable. He gathered up paperwork, Andrea's cookbooks, his computer, and other items and lugged them upstairs. Glancing out the upstairs bedroom window, he noticed through the spring-leafed trees that angry, brown waters were swirling toward the house. Soon they were flowing under the house, raised on stilts about 14 feet aboveground. The modern structure was designed for that eventuality, but it had never happened.

Friends began calling; so did Andrea. They were urging White to leave. Neighbors called, said they were worried; from their vantage point, it looked like water was engulfing the house, they said. Get out, they said.

"They were pretty adamant," White recalled in his usual understated way.

He stayed a while longer, stuffing towels around doors and moving more items upstairs and into the attic. "I thought I'd be okay," he said. "I was on the swim team in high school, so I thought I could swim out if I had to."

Between noon and about 1 o'clock, he heard the water gurgling beneath the floor. When it started bursting through electrical sockets and ripping up floorboards, he knew his time was up. No more bravado, swim team or not. With water up to his ankles, he went upstairs, found his hiking poles and began stuffing a few clothes into a backpack. He pulled on khaki shorts and a T-shirt and boots he wears on hunting trips. Pole in one hand and a black briefcase full of work documents in the other, he stepped into the chest-deep, coffee-colored waters.

"I was in the middle of a bayou that was moving fast, the fastest I had ever seen it move," he recalled. "When it jumped the banks, there was a very strong westbound current, knocking down fences, carrying away yard furniture."

White made it to the neighbors' house and for the next couple of weeks, between dealing with contractors and clean-up crews, helped Mayor Turner and County Judge Emmett deal with the region's unprecedented catastrophe. His experience with Katrina, Rita, and Ike came in handy when it came to negotiating with FEMA, the Red Cross, and large donors from around the country.

"Neighbors helping neighbors was exemplary and wonderful, but no surprise," he said. "I know how we've helped each other in prior disasters."

———————

Houston on Saturday night was beneath the full force of a major thunderstorm band that struck the west side of the city and moved through central Houston dumping four-plus inches of rain—every hour. As tens of thousands of Houstonians began to realize how dire their situation was, roads were becoming vehicle-deep torrents of water. Bayous began spilling over into nearby residential areas.

Unlike Katrina, which left New Orleans' most vulnerable residents homeless and bereft, Harvey saturated vast swaths of Houston, a 650-square-mile metropolis larger than Rhode Island. Few neighborhoods were left untouched, forcing rich and poor, suburbanites and city-dwellers of all backgrounds into the streets of one of the most diverse cities in America.

In wealthy communities on the west side, working-class communities on the east, and neighborhoods in between, water was rising. Residents watched with foreboding as it advanced like a malevolent force. Like an unstoppable liquid wrath, it insinuated itself into yards, onto porches, and then into houses. The rising water was active, sinister—warping floorboards, soaking carpets, and destroying furniture, clothes, valuable belongings, irreplaceable heirlooms.

Those in multistory homes or apartments retreated to a second floor. Floodwaters followed. Cars parked in driveways disappeared under instant lakes. In apartment complex parking lots, waves of water lifted vehicles and shoved them like Matchbox toys up against apartment walls.

People were driving into what they assumed were puddles on streets and roadways, only to have their cars stall. Cold, brackish waters rose above windows and poured into their vehicles from the floorboard. Some could not get out.

Batool Qasem, 76, died Saturday afternoon after driving into high water and leaving her car. She was found floating in floodwaters near her vehicle, not far from Buffalo Bayou. Travis Lynn Callihan, 45, was pronounced dead at an area hospital on Monday. He perished after exiting a vehicle and falling into floodwaters. Agnes Stanley, 89, drowned Sunday morning in her home. Charles Ray James, 65, was found floating in high waters on a residential street on Tuesday. He had been trying to reach his 90-year-old mother at the height of the storm.

Manuel Acevedo, 67, was found in an alleyway after floodwaters receded in East Houston. The father of four daughters had gone to get a truck to rescue his bedridden wife Dianne but never made it back. Andrew Pasek, 25, died on Tuesday after stepping on live electrical wires concealed by floodwaters in northwest Harris County. His family said he was trying to rescue his sister's cat from the home she had evacuated. The body of Keisha Monique

Williams, 32, was found on Wednesday after floodwaters receded. The nurse and single mother of two had gone back to her home to get her daughters' new school clothes and their dogs.

Jill Renick, 48, drowned at her workplace at the Omni Houston Hotel, where she and her dog had gone before the storm so she could help guests. She called the front desk on Sunday to say she was trapped in an elevator—and was never heard from again. The hotel was being evacuated as floodwaters entered the building, and initial efforts to locate her were unsuccessful. Her body was discovered more than a week later in a ceiling area of the basement near some elevators.

As water rose in neighborhoods throughout Houston, local officials began warning flood victims to get to their roofs, not their attics, and to stay on the 911 line until they could get through. Perched on a roof for hours at a time, they were wet, cold, and in danger of sliding off. Within a few hours, 911 would be overwhelmed.

All through Sunday and into Monday, thousands of people were abandoning their inundated homes and apartments. Carrying children, pets, plastic bags full of whatever they could grab as they fled, they slogged through swirling brown water toward rescue. U.S. Coast Guard helicopters rescued residents off rooftops. Texas Governor Greg Abbott called out 3,000 National Guard members. The federal government declared Harris County a disaster area.

As Sunday-evening darkness settled in, the rain kept coming down. Residents of a sprawling, middle-class master-planned community called Cinco Ranch were advised to evacuate.

"We're all trapped in here. The entire front of the subdivision is completely flooded," resident Eli Magana told the *Houston Chronicle*. "There's no way to get out, and there's no way to get to a shelter."

In the Galveston area, more than a dozen nursing home residents were rescued after a viral picture showed a group of elderly people in a Dickinson facility sitting in waist-high water, according to the *Chronicle*.

Harris County Constable Alan Rosen confronted a similar situation. In Meyerland, the Seven Acres Jewish Senior Care Services, an elder care facility on the north bank of Brays Bayou, not only was flooding but had run out of fuel for its generators. With 300 people living at Seven Acres, a number with dementia, Rosen was determined to prevent a repeat of what happened in New Orleans during Hurricane Katrina, when elderly people were abandoned. He happened to know a fuel distributor across town and was able to retrieve the fuel in a Hummer, make his way back to the facility, and get the generators running again. Residents did not have to evacuate.

By then the calls coming in to Rosen's office and to 911 were so overwhelming, he had to institute something of a triage regimen. "We started focusing on people with medical issues, people in wheelchairs, people who needed oxygen or dialysis," he recalled. "We had to rescue people who were in big peril."

"It's catastrophic, unprecedented, epic—whatever adjective you want to use," said Patrick Blood, a National Weather Service meteorologist.

"This is pretty much like Day 2," Mayor Turner reminded his fellow Houstonians during a Sunday-afternoon press conference. "There will be Day 3, there will be Day 4, and there may be Day 5.

It's important for Houstonians to be very patient. Let's not get storm fatigue."

Some version of what Jennifer and Jim Dean's family went through was a familiar experience to countless Houstonians throughout the city. The Deans lived in a neighborhood of modest brick homes and spacious backyards in Pearland, a fast-growing suburb just south of Houston. They were relieved to have made it through the weekend of nearly nonstop downpours with minor street flooding and some water in their driveway.

They assumed the worst was over, so they decided to stay put, not evacuate, but Monday brought another day of torrential rain that simply would not stop. Their neighborhood Facebook page was busy with updates and advice; the Weather Channel blared nonstop.

Monday afternoon, Jim, a bearded 46-year-old who wore wire-rimmed glasses and one of a dozen Astros caps he owns, decided to take a nap. When he woke a couple of hours later, Jennifer had a message for him: no more naps. The day had taken an alarming turn.

"It's still pouring rain, and it's coming up to the house," Jim, a sales associate for a construction supply company, recalled some weeks later. The family, including grown daughter Haleigh and the Deans' two young sons, started brainstorming. They decided to seal themselves inside the house by duct-taping doors, plugging weep holes, and creating sandbags out of damp towels and plastic bags (an idea Jennifer got from the Internet). They moved the cars into the garage and parked their SUV sideways on the driveway close to the house. They had food, water, power, and beer.

Their plan worked for a while. Jim and Haleigh, 24, spent Monday evening watching the Weather Channel, while Jennifer stayed with sons Wyatt and Hudson in the master bedroom trying to keep their minds off the storm. About 9:00 p.m., father and daughter noticed their cat Pyro batting at something on the ground near the wall. It was water.

The duct-taped doors had held, but the Deans weren't able to seal the entire bottom of the house. The floodwaters began seeping in through the walls—like the Blob, Jim said.

"Once it started coming in, it came in really fast," Jennifer recalled.

At press conference on Sunday evening, Mayor Turner said that 5,500 people had made their way to city- and county-run shelters. Many more were expected, he said. Houston Police Chief Art Acevedo said that his department had fielded 56,000 calls to 911 since the previous Friday and that more than 2,000 people had been rescued.

"Reports of people getting into attic to escape floodwater—do not do so unless you have an ax or means to break through onto your roof," Acevedo wrote on Twitter.

Back in Pearland, "the Blob" scaling the walls of the Deans' house inched steadily upward. Jim Dean made the decision to evacuate. After a few phone calls, they found a place to stay at Jennifer Dean's boss's house; the boss was staying elsewhere. Jennifer had a key, the house was nearby, and it was dry.

But they were marooned in their neighborhood. Boats had nosed into the neighborhood and were plying the streets rescuing people. The Deans flashed the front porch light repeatedly to draw their attention. Two men in a passing boat said they were on their way to another rescue but promised to come back for them soon.

They did, docking near the Deans' front door, at the intersection of Apple Springs Drive and Neches River Street. The boys, Haleigh, two cats, Cash the family dog (named for Johnny Cash), and Jennifer and Jim Dean found a spot in the flat-bottom boat. They pulled away slowly, so as not to cause a wake that would push even more water into homes. The Deans took some clothes, their passports, Jim's ammo bag, and two pistols. Nothing else. It was dark in the familiar neighborhood, dark and foreboding. The heavy rain would not stop.

Leaving the boat to clamber into a truck that would take them to the boss's house, Jennifer realized that the key to the house where they were headed was on her keychain back at their house. Jim, wearing mud boots and an Astros cap, waded the four blocks back home through the dark and rain. The cold, stinking flood-waters rose to his chest. He opened the front door, and a torrent of water rushed into the living room with him. He spotted the ice chest bobbing in the water, cans of cold beer still inside.

"At this point, I'm done," he recalled. "I give up. We're screwed. I get the keys—and a cold beer."

CHAPTER 6

Saving Lives

My Facebook addiction has finally paid off.
KERI HENRY, WHO USED SOCIAL MEDIA TO COORDINATE
RESCUE OPERATIONS

A new workweek dawned, although a great many Houstonians weren't going to work, at least not their normal jobs. Now, three days after Harvey first made landfall, additional threats loomed for thousands of Houstonians living in upscale neighborhoods on the west side of town. Addicks and Barker Reservoirs, built in the 1940s, were filling up. As the *Chronicle* reported, a civil research engineer named Aaron Byrd, working in the U.S. Army Engineer Research and Development Center, had helped develop an inundation modeling technology some years earlier that was capable of forecasting flood depths up to five days in advance.

The U.S. Army Corps of Engineers had relied on it during Hurricanes Irene in 2011 and Sandy in 2012. Byrd and his team had used it a few days earlier to monitor Harvey as it hit the Texas coast. At that point, the forecast included in the corps' bulletin on

Addicks and Barker was relatively unremarkable: 10 to 15 inches of rain. No overtopping expected.

By Monday afternoon—64 hours after landfall—Byrd had a model running that took into account the flooding already occurring, the rainfall, the releases, and the forecast. At that point, he told the *Chronicle*, the flooding would not just be "one home here, one home there. It was going to be miles and miles of homes."

The corps asked Byrd to run a second model. People had built homes inside the boundaries of the two reservoirs, he was told. Some of those homes would start flooding within hours, once the flood pool reached 103.4 feet in Addicks. At 9:00 a.m., it was at 103.37 feet.

Addicks was built to hold water as high as 108 feet above sea level before it flows around the north end of the dam; above 111.5 feet, the water would top the emergency spillway. Some of the homes would be nearly 8 feet underwater if the reservoir level reached the spillway.

Barker, the other reservoir, had the same limitations. The emergency spillway was at 105.1 feet. The lowest homes were at 97.1 feet.

The corps wanted to know which homes were going to flood and where, in order to get the information to first responders. Byrd pulled up Google Earth and was astounded to see row after row of homes in the flood pools, thousands of them. He scanned the area near the Addicks spillway. A commercial center and sprawling subdivisions with two-story homes had been constructed at the bottom of the spillway.

"How did they get permission to build there?" he wondered.

They flooded, but not because the reservoirs failed. The corps made the agonizing decision to allow more water to pour into the bayou, already way beyond capacity. As Susan Carroll of the *Chronicle* put it, "the corps had finally faced it's Sophie's Choice with Harvey: release water during a monster storm and doom houses along the bayou, or risk letting the water flow from around the ends of the dams and over the emergency spillways—perhaps triggering a much bigger disaster."

The corps opted for release. Tons of water invaded neighborhoods. And stayed for weeks.

"The trillion gallons of water that Harvey dumped on Harris County during four days in August—enough to fill the Astrodome more than 3,300 times—revealed the downside of Houston's dynamic economy," the *Chronicle* noted. "The region's growth formula, which relies heavily on abundant, cheap housing and lax regulation, suddenly had a death toll in the dozens and a price tag in the billions."

On the east side of town, home to the largest concentration of oil refineries, tank farms, and petrochemical plants in the world, yet another threat loomed. Environmentalists had been warning for years that if the Houston Ship Channel took a direct hit from a hurricane or some other natural disaster, the results would be catastrophic. Imagine scenes that would challenge Hollywood's most daring designers of the apocalypse: fiery explosions. The spreading sheen of oil poisoning the ship channel. Deadly chemicals rendering the Gulf a dead zone. Residents of nearby neighborhoods breathing in deadly fumes. Empty houses, their residents gone forever.

Real life, not a spectacular movie, would endanger thousands of people. The nation's economy also would suffer catastrophically. Harvey and the flood offered previews.

In Houston's Manchester neighborhood near the mouth of the Houston Ship Channel, Harvey's floodwaters triggered the release of toxic emissions and thousands of gallons of petroleum spills. A storage tank roof collapsed at Valero Energy's East Houston Refinery, spewing some 235,000 pounds of toxic vapors and other pollutants into the atmosphere. Manchester's residents, primarily poor Hispanic families, have had to live for years with little information about what they were breathing. During Harvey, it was no different.

In the working-class suburb of Crosby, along the densely developed channel, dangerous chemical fires erupted. Arkema, a French multinational company that manufactures chemicals used to create plastic products, lost control of its facility after six feet of floodwaters cut the power and destroyed its backup generators. The power failure knocked out a cooling system crucial for storing volatile organic peroxides, which risk explosion as the temperature rises. The chemicals were moved to refrigerated trailers, but trailers also began to fail.

On Tuesday, four days after Harvey came ashore near Rockport, officials ordered the evacuation of everyone within 1.5 miles of the Arkema plant. The first fire broke out early Thursday, sending plumes of ominous black smoke spiraling into the air. Law enforcement officers and medical staff arrived on the scene and doubled over from the fumes. They began vomiting and gasping for air.

Two additional trailers caught fire on Friday. Two days later, the Houston Police Department's bomb squad entered the area and detonated the remaining six trailers to burn out the remaining chemicals. Residents of about 300 homes near the plant had to leave. More than 30 people, including law enforcement, ended up in the hospital. As bad as it was, it could have been so much worse.

—————————

The rain continued to fall and Houstonians were finding novel ways to help flood victims. Alan Rosen, the Harris County constable, started relying on social media, since 911 was overwhelmed. He soon realized that Facebook and Twitter were more reliable.

Keri Henry, a 36-year-old mother of two young daughters living in an upscale central Houston enclave, made the same discovery. She realized she could turn her Facebook addiction into a life-saving tool. Her family was safe and dry, but she still wanted to find a way to help. As she watched the flooding crisis unfold in Facebook postings, as she agonized at so many people begging for help, she grabbed a notebook and started jotting down names and addresses.

She quickly accumulated the names of dozens of flood victims from nearby neighborhoods and starting seeking people with boats and sharing information. Messages starting pouring in. Each time she glanced at her phone, it seemed, someone else had tagged her with information about someone in trouble.

Within hours, she was working her own dispatch operation from her living room with an iPhone, a laptop, her notebook, and her Facebook page. She worked frantically to connect a growing list of boat owners who wanted to help with families who desperately needed it. Her ad hoc rescue organization morphed over the next couple of days, involving friends near and far and people she didn't know and probably would never meet.

"I started to get into my own virtual world," she recalled.

Hers was a single rescue group in a sprawling city full of similar operations seeking to help those in need. Many of these informal groups started on neighborhood Facebook groups and message boards, others on Twitter. Some used the Austin-based app Zello, designed to work where cell phone signals are weak and useful in conflict zones around the world. During Harvey, as many as 7,000 people per minute were downloading the app, according to the company. It was a sign of the massive mobilization effort that was growing by the minute across southeast Texas.

Other sites, like Houstonsheltermap.com, started as spreadsheets before launching as interactive maps offering people real-time information about the city's shelters, such as whether pets were accepted and what types of donations were needed. Some assisted in getting food to shelters as well.

"People just like me and my tiny little organization were forming everywhere," Henry said.

The rain continued and the online pleas for help kept coming. "Everything was dire, dire, dire for the first three days," she said.

There was the man with 10 teenagers. The elderly couple, one with a broken hip. A friend with a two-week-old baby who needed to be evacuated. People were stuck in homes, on roofs, in apartments.

Henry worked endless hours and hated to go to sleep for even a little while. "Wondering how many people I didn't save while trying to sleep, back at it. Please pray for clarity, organization, efficiency," she wrote on her page.

"I HAVE BOATS," Henry posted at 10:19 p.m. Sunday. "I need people to private message me CURRENT people in need, SPECIFI-CALLY in Braeswood/Meyerland!!"

With water inexorably rising throughout the region in the early morning hours, the stream of desperate messages kept coming.

"Two elderly people trapped in a one story on their kitchen counters since noon," one woman wrote, providing an address. "They are in desperate need of help."

"Seven people trapped in second floor," another posted. "They have been tapped for over 9 hours and running low on phone battery power."

As people continued to message and tag Henry on Facebook seeking help, two friends helped her transfer the names of boaters and victims to an Excel spreadsheet. At this point, she recalled, her name had spread online and she was receiving messages from people in nearby towns. Boaters arriving from as far away as Oklahoma, Arkansas, and Florida found their way to her on Facebook. Where should we go? they wanted to know. Who can we help?

With connections developing online across the Houston region, rescue groups began to merge, allowing them to trade resources and tips. One new partner overseeing a fleet of boats had used Google Docs to create an online emergency help form that people in need would fill for rescuers. It included vital information, shared widely, about location and phone number, but also additional details such as whether a person had any pets.

Boaters, meanwhile, were placed on a group text with strict guidelines for communication, which would direct them to "hot spots" around the city that were constantly changing, Henry said. It didn't take long for defined roles in the organization to emerge.

On Monday, three friends calling themselves "Houston Harvey Rescue" launched a dispatch website that rescuers and volunteers began using immediately. "We created houstonharveyrescue.com in under 3 hours, in a leaky office, with intermittent power a 2GB server and had absolutely no idea it would lead to over 7,600 active rescues in thanks to over 8,000 brave rescuers, dispatchers, and volunteers," the site says.

"I just felt so helpless," one of the site's founders, Matt Marchetti, told CBS affiliate KHOU.

An open-source model, the website allowed users to add a flood victim's name to a Google map if they needed rescuing. The location of the rescue was designated by a pin on the map, which changed color according to the urgency of the rescue. After the victim was rescued, the pin was removed, giving rescuers across the city a real-time view of needs around Houston.

"It was organized chaos," said Secunda Joseph, a Houston activist who joined strangers to compile spreadsheets with the names of flood victims in northeast Houston. Many of those on the list, she said, were older people who didn't have access to smartphones and were unable to reach rescuers while they were marooned on their roof or standing in waist-deep water. Without their younger relatives organizing to find them help online, they may have died, Joseph said.

A number did die. During the first week of September, Harris County announced that the morgue was nearing capacity and needed help from the state. As the *Houston Chronicle* noted, the announcement sounded like something from a horror movie, but the heartbreaking stories were all too real. They kept coming.

- My grandfather's grandfather clock, built in 1912 to sit on a mantel or a shelf, hadn't run for years. I found a clock-repair shop online and took it in to see if it was fixable. That's where I met a congenial man named Alexander Kwoksum Sung, 64, an immigrant from China whose tiny place of business was in a dingy South Houston strip center where the signs on most storefronts were *en español*. He had been in business for 30 years. "We make things tick," a small sign on the glass front door announced.

  Accu-Tyme Clock Repair, between a humble *panaderia* and a two-chair beauty salon, was a jam-packed welter of stately grandfather clocks. To get from the front door to the counter in back required weaving through what resembled a jumbled downtown skyline of clocks taller than a person's head. Yelp respondents complained that he took too long to complete their repairs, even though many commented on his kindness and courtesy. A perfectionist, admirers said.

  I complained too. My repair job took months, but eventually Sung had my old clock keeping time and chiming just as it had in my grandparents' farmhouse parlor more than a century ago. I didn't know until weeks later that the small strip center took on water the weekend Harvey hit. I didn't know that Sung chose to ride out the flood inside his shop. That's where he drowned, surrounded by all those clocks.

- Houston Police Sergeant Steve Perez, 60, got ready for work on Sunday morning, even though his wife, Cheryl, begged him not to. "I've got work to do," the 34-year HPD veteran told her. He assured her he would be all right.

Perez drowned in his car in floodwaters on Sunday morning. After driving for more than two hours trying to find a way to reach police headquarters in downtown Houston, he accidentally drove into high water in an underpass and couldn't get out of his car. His body was found days later.

Houston Police Chief Art Acevedo, in tears, told mourners at Perez's funeral that his death was symbolic of all the sacrifices Houston made as it bore the brunt of the storm.

"When he drove into the water that morning, God was there to catch him," the chief said. "He served as an absolute testament of the excellence of the men and women in blue."

- On Sunday, Sammy Saldivar was trying to drive his family to safety when raging floodwaters swept his van off the road near Greens Bayou in east Houston. He was able to swim to safety, but the others didn't make it. His parents, Belia and Manuel Saldivar, ages 81 and 84, drowned. So did their four great-grandchildren: Devorah "Devy," 16; Dominic, 14; Xavier, 8; Daisy, 6.

- On Monday, five volunteer rescuers set out in a small boat to help evacuate a wheelchair-bound neighbor in the Northshore area of Houston. Not long afterward, they had to take to the water when the swift current in Greens Bayou swept them toward a power line. Jorge Raul Perez, 33; Yahir Rubio-Vizuet, 25; his brother Benjamin Vizuet, 33; and Gustavo Hernandez Rodriguez, 40, drowned. The Houston Fire Department found the bodies of Perez and Rubio-Vizuet the next day.

The incessant rain continued to torment Houston. The tales of bravery, heroism, and kindness, of Houstonians trying to help any way they could also continued. They risked danger to themselves, not only drowning or electrocution but also potentially fatal illnesses. Sewers had backed up and those who stood in water tearing out drywall or ripping out soggy carpet risked infection. One woman died of flesh-eating bacteria (flood-related necrotizing fasciitis) that invaded her body through a small cut on her leg while she waded through fetid waters.

Jeremiah Richard and his six-year-old son climbed through a window of their apartment complex, clambered into a helicopter's dangling basket, and were ferried to safety. "We thank God. We thank God," Richard told a KTRK-TV reporter, as he and Jeremiah Jr. were set down on a deserted Houston freeway. They walked away with only backpacks stuffed with belongings. "This is all we got," Richard said.

With a riverboat captain's aplomb, 15-year-old Declan Connor, shirtless and wearing a brown baseball cap, piloted his family's fishing boat through the streets of his Meyerland neighborhood with his brother and a friend. They peered into the murky waters as they puttered through the neighborhood, on the lookout for submerged cars and downed trees. The teenagers rescued dozens of people.

One of Constable Rosen's deputies saw a man wading down the middle of a flooded street suddenly disappear. He had stepped into an open manhole. The deputy went in after him and managed to lift him out of the rushing underground stream before both were washed away.

Using tree branches, umbrellas, and even tennis rackets, a group of people worked off and on for several days to rescue Mexican free-tailed bats after rising waters inundated their roost under a bridge over Buffalo Bayou. Some 250,000 live under the bridge, one of the largest urban colonies in Texas. Their mass ascensions at dusk have gained popularity over the years among residents who gather on the bridge or sit on the grassy slopes.

Alicia Plunkett, 21, was walking across the bridge on Saturday when she saw some of the furry, little creatures floating by in the rising brown waters. She plucked one out of the fast-moving waters, then another and another. Others helped over the next few days.

"You could hear them in there," Plunkett told the *Houston Chronicle*. To her, their usual tweeting sounded like screams. "They couldn't get out."

Once roads were passable, Houstonians whose homes were unaffected by the flood took to driving through neighborhoods, along streets that had become canyons lined 10-feet-high with water-soaked and ruined belongings. Day after day, strangers stopped to help when they encountered residents hauling what had been their possessions out to the curb. The odor of backed-up sewage, mildew, mold, and damp debris didn't deter them.

At the downtown George R. Brown Convention Center, evacuees were streaming in, some 10,000 eventually. Many were large families, carrying backpacks and rolling suitcases. Many arrived barefoot, bringing nothing but the clothes on their backs.

Christella Gomez told the *Texas Tribune* she packed up and left her downtown area home with her two children at the insistence of a neighbor. Floodwaters from nearby Buffalo Bayou had overwhelmed her housing complex.

Across town, Virginia Hammond made her way to the GRB as floodwaters began to enter her northwest Houston home. She told the *Tribune* it had flooded three times in the past nine years. During another historic flood in the city last year, she found herself trapped inside with her two granddaughters as her home filled with nearly three feet of water.

"I kinda felt like it was gonna happen, so we left," she said in an interview Sunday afternoon. "The streets were flooding and the bayou was up to the top."

Longtime Houstonians Anne Whitlock and Michael Skelly were among hundreds of volunteers trying to help their fellow Houstonians at shelters. At the GRB, they met two families of Mexican immigrants (undocumented) who had fled their apartment because of rising water. The couple invited the evacuees, including two young girls, home with them—they live in a restored firehouse—and on social media encouraged their fellow Houstonians to do the same. A number did just that.

Ryan Slattery, a 34-year-old designer, hangs out with a group of about 20 pals, young men and women who primarily work in politics and public policy and spend a lot of their off-hours together. A day before the storm struck Texas, they got a group text from one of their number who worked on Mayor Turner's staff. He wanted to know if they'd be ready to assist at the GRB if a shelter was activated there. The answer was a unanimous yes.

Slattery took on the task of setting up a shower area, one that

could offer flood victims a modicum of normality in their trauma-
tized lives.

"It was really an impressive undertaking done by a bunch of
political hacks who didn't really understand the gravity of what
they had to do," he said. "We were just there to lend a hand....It
was a great group of people working together during one of the
most extreme situations anyone can imagine."

One of his unofficial chores was to keep National Guards he
was working alongside supplied with "coffee and Copenhagen."
The first day he worked with them, he called in ahead, asking what
they might need.

"I had to stop at two corner stores just to get all of the energy
drinks they wanted," he recalled, laughing. He found that with
coffee and chewing tobacco, you can get just about anything done.
"They did an incredible job," he said.

Slattery's motto was "Be polite, get shit done." He often started
at six in the morning and was still working 15 hours later. He was
helping his neighbors, fellow Houstonians who "had a good run of
bad luck." They just wanted to go home, although Slattery remembers one of them, a young woman, who was able to go home after a
couple of days and was back a few days later. Helping.

"I think Houston is more of a melded city than most," Slattery
said. "There are longtime Houstonians and new residents who
bring the best of where they came from."

Like Slattery's National Guard partners, rescue workers and
other emergency personnel were running on adrenaline, caffeine,
junk food, and little sleep—some of them working to help others
even as their own homes were flooded.

Cesar Temores, a native Houstonian, was ensconced in Harris

County's Emergency Operations Center, trying to help frantic callers and tend to other duties when he got word that his Spring neighborhood north of Houston was taking on water. His wife, Dolores, and daughters, Isabella, 8, and Mia, 2, were safe at her mother's house, but Rascal, the family dog, had been left behind in the backyard. Their home had never flooded in the 13 years they had lived there.

Temores couldn't abandon his duties; he really didn't want to. He wanted to help—and was one of the few emergency personnel who was bilingual. He could hear the terror in the voices of callers, their tears. "Get to the roof," he had to tell a number of them, warning them not to go into an attic where they could be trapped. He did his best to assure them that help was on the way, but he knew he couldn't guarantee it.

He was on a break Sunday afternoon when his neighbors called again with the awful news that his home had flooded. "It hit me hard. You realize everything you have is gone," he recalled.

But Temores soon went back to work and remained at his post until Wednesday. He told only one colleague what had happened. They both cried.

"I took a second to reflect, then I got back to helping people worse off than me," he said. "I heard so many sad stories, tears, babies crying....Sunday was a very long day."

Temores left the command center Wednesday morning after his boss, Judge Emmett, urged him to go home and be with his family. He returned to devastation—some 70 percent of the 240 homes in the neighborhood had flooded. Some, including his, took on three feet of water, while others had as much as six feet, almost to the ceiling.

As he stared at the devastation all around him, he heard a noise—a bark in the distance. "I thought, 'Oh God!'" Two houses down, atop a pile of debris inside a garage was Rascal, skinny and bedraggled after days of no food, but alive.

"I was so happy. It made things so much better," he said. "I was real emotional. It gave me hope."

CHAPTER 7

Harvey and the Astros' Home Run

.@JoseAltuve27: *I feel like I owe Houston something.*
All they've given me for 6 years, supporting me every day.
Now is my time to show up.

The hottest team in baseball was in Anaheim, California, for a series with the Angels when Harvey besieged its hometown. The Astros watched on TV as their city drowned, as volunteers did everything they could to rescue neighbors and strangers. Aside from calls to loved ones back home, there was nothing they could do to help. They were professional baseball players, paid to entertain fans in "the Big A," the Angels stadium a few miles from Disneyland.

How the Astros would get back to Houston, when they would get back to Houston, nobody was at all sure. Finishing up with the Angels, they packed up to head for home, only to be diverted to Dallas–Fort Worth, 300 miles to the north. Next up was a three-game series at home in Houston against their in-state rivals, the Texas Rangers.

Since nobody would be playing baseball in the Bayou City any-time soon, and since the team happened to be in the Dallas–Fort Worth area anyway, the Astros suggested swapping out a September series between the two teams in Arlington with the series in Houston. No way, the Rangers said. The team said it didn't want to inconvenience fans who had purchased tickets for the games in September.

"You've got a major storm that's disrupted everything. We went to the Rangers and said, 'Hey, let's switch series. You guys have our home series, we'll take your home series,'" Astros President Reid Ryan said. "They rejected that and didn't want to do that."

As Ryan (son of Nolan) explained, the Rangers insisted on play-ing the next three days at their place, but didn't want to trade out the series in Houston toward the end of the season. They wanted all six games at their park.

"We had to look at our players' best interest, and we had to look at the integrity of the schedule," Ryan said.

Social media blasted the Rangers as uncaring bums. A tweet by Astro pitcher Lance McCullers Jr. summed up the incredu-lous response to the Ranger's obstinance. He tweeted, "Classy as always, should be absolutely ashamed. Greed never takes off days, apparently. Stay strong #Htown! We hope to be home soon."

McCullers's boss, Astros owner Jim Crane, was a bit more measured. Asked by *Sports Business Daily*, whether the decision changed the Astros' relationship with the Rangers long term, he said, "It is what it is. I've told anybody that if the situation was reversed, I would have [switched the series]. I would have given them a break. We're just playing baseball here, folks. It's just three baseball games, not a life-and-death situation. You can't even put them in the same perspective. We're just trying to do what's best for the team and what's best for the city."

So, instead of playing the Rangers in Houston or in Arlington, the vagabond Astros were dispatched to Tropicana Field in St. Petersburg, Florida, home of the Tampa Bay Rays. They would play their six-game "home stand" against the Rangers and the Mets a thousand miles from home, a thousand miles from their families.

The players were seeing the same distressing images from back home that everybody else was seeing. The Astros were inundated by cable news images from Houston. George Springer did not know if his home had survived. (It had, but the house was unreachable for days.) Charlie Morton's wife and kids were stranded. José Altuve's home was unscathed, but, like the Morton family, his wife and infant were inside and unable to leave because of floodwaters in their neighborhood. Players couldn't resist checking their iPhones in the dugout. They incessantly watched the Weather Channel in their hotel rooms at night.

"How long do I have to play with this on my heart?" Altuve asked A. J. Hinch at one point.

"I don't know," Hinch told him.

"That's not easy to ask your players, 'José, now, go out and get your normal two and three hits. Be the three-hole hitter. Play hard. And deliver us a win,' Hinch said later.

"And we did. We won a couple of games along that stretch. But if you want to humanize baseball, look at that story. And it will show you what these guys go through daily in their personal lives that leads to the professional lives. And on top of that, I think we were able to really keep in perspective what was going on in Houston."

Hinch had tears in his eyes when he told reporters that his neighbors had rescued a baby from the floodwaters and that he wished he could have been there helping them.

Crane saw that his players were beginning to panic. He starting sending people from the Astros' front office to check on the players' families.

Marwin Gonzalez's wife, Noel, and their two children were in their apartment on an upper floor of a building near downtown. They couldn't get out either, and Noel was expecting. She would deliver a baby boy shortly after the first game of the American League Championship Series, a 2–1 Astros victory over the New York Yankees in which Marwin would make a magnificent throw from left field to cut down a runner at home plate.

"I am thinking of naming him José Altuve or Dallas Keuchel," Gonzales joked in Spanish after the game, shortly before rushing off to the hospital. (The couple settled on the name Blake.)

Whatever was happening back home, it was baseball weather in sunny St. Petersburg, but the atmosphere was all wrong. The Tropicana stands were mostly empty. The "home" team from Texas dressed in the visitors' clubhouse, while the "road" team from Texas wore their white home uniforms. In the first game, the Rangers pounded the tired and distracted Astros 12–2, in front of an announced crowd of 3,485 die-hard baseball fans (or sun worshippers). The Astros lost the second game 8–1 before salvaging a victory in the third.

In the bottom of the first inning of the third game, second base umpire Joe West kicked out Hinch. The manager had contested a double play called against the Astros on a strikeout, after which Alex Bregman was ruled to have obstructed Rangers catcher Brett

Nicholas's throw as he tried to catch a stealing Springer. Hinch was animated but civil in arguing with home plate umpire Chris Segal before West, the crew chief, injected himself into the tiff and gave Hinch the ol' heave-ho. As the game dragged on, a clubhouse-bound Hinch had time to wonder what his Astros were doing in Florida in the first place.

"It was very tough, and a lot of guys, their wives were here [in Houston], their families were here, kids," McCullers would recall in the coming weeks. "It was very tough for us to be away. In those difficult days, we wanted to come home. We wanted to see our families, make sure everything was okay. We wanted to help the city of Houston as much as we could."

"[The worst part] was probably the unknown," Astros reliever Will Harris told Michael Bauman of MLB.com. "We were in Tampa not knowing what the situation was back home, if our houses were underwater. Just being here and not being able to see it. Driving in when we landed on Thursday was surreal, driving through the city and seeing the aftermath of the storm."

Harris, a Louisiana native and LSU alum, still had vivid memories of Hurricane Katrina "It was my senior year of college, and my roommate's family lost their house in New Orleans and lived with us that whole school year," he told Baumann. "You see the resiliency of people. You kind of do what you have to do after it's over. You put your head down and keep living and work your way back. It's not easy, but people do that."

The Astros were resigned to playing the Mets in Florida, as well, before Houston Mayor Sylvester Turner intervened. He called Astros owner Crane. "Bring 'em home," he urged. "Help us get this city back to normal."

"We feel that the Astros playing this weekend will provide a much-needed boost for our city," the mayor said in a statement. "With all of the difficulties that many of our citizens are facing, the games will provide opportunities for families to start returning to some aspect of normal life."

Later, Turner would say: "This is what we do in Houston. We help our neighbors out. We play ball."

Scheduled to embark on a 10-game West Coast road trip on the other side of their "home stand" in Florida, the Astros didn't need persuading. Plus, Minute Maid was in good shape, thanks to a maintenance crew who stayed at the park night and day during the storm, racing to plug leaks in the cavernous facility whenever they were discovered.

At 3:18 p.m. on Wednesday, Ryan tweeted a picture of Minute Maid. The park appeared to be unscathed under partly cloudy skies. He wrote, "View from my office today. Minute Maid is ready. Astros return Saturday. We are accepting donations at the gates for victims."

The team also announced it would be providing 5,000 free tickets to first responders, volunteers, and evacuees.

The Mets players had to agree to the schedule change, and they did. They not only agreed to play a doubleheader on Saturday, but several players also visited neighborhoods to help with cleanup efforts.

So they were coming home for a doubleheader against the Mets on Saturday, then a regularly scheduled series finale on Sunday. The first game of the series was originally scheduled for Friday night, but Ryan reminded league officials that the players hadn't seen their families for days.

"Our players are human beings first and foremost," he said in a statement. "They have been away from their families and neighborhoods during this time of need. We want them to reunite with their families. They also know the role they play in providing hope and encouragement to our entire community—they are proud to represent Houston."

When the Astros plane from Tampa began to descend over Houston, "you could have heard a pin drop," one of the passengers recalled. Every player was peering out of windows at the watery devastation below. On the team bus into downtown from George Bush Intercontinental Airport, players stared out at mountains of debris lining residential streets, at damaged houses and buildings, and still-standing water. It was a sobering experience for them all.

Hinch said he got texts from several players asking what they could do to help their city. The day after they got home, several got a firsthand look at the pain and suffering their fellow Houstonians were experiencing. More than a dozen spent their day off at the vast shelter organized on the fly for thousands of temporary evacuees at the George R. Brown Convention Center, two blocks from Minute Maid Park. The huge glass-and-concrete building, with its white walls, blue trusses, and curved red vents, resembles an ocean liner docked between two hotels downtown. It had been remodeled a few months earlier, in time for Houston to host Super Bowl LI; the remodeling was designed to make the building more open and welcoming. No one could have imagined how welcoming it would turn out to be just a few months later.

In just two days, the mayor's office had transformed the GRB into a veritable village for 10,000 Houstonians who had no place else to go. TV satellite trucks from around the country surrounded the building. Traffic along adjacent streets slowed to a standstill as Houstonians in pickup trucks unloaded plastic bags of donations. People on foot brought boxes of diapers, pillows, blankets, dog food, just about anything imaginable that people would need in an emergency. Buses and open-bed trucks continued to bring in wet and exhausted evacuees. As Harris County Constable Alan Rosen recalled, many seemed to be in a daze, almost in shock.

Volunteers from Houston and elsewhere stood in line to sign up for opportunities to help. Many had been inspired by the dramatic rescues they had seen on TV; they wanted to do their part.

Inside the building, a clean, well-lighted place in the midst of dank misery, the operation was noisy and bustling, but organized. Families clustered together on cots or stood in line for clothing or food or diapers, whatever they needed. Babies slept. Evacuees with pets had their own separate area. Volunteers organized activities for kids, helped sort donated clothing. Others helped new arrivals fill out FEMA forms. Doctors and nurses looked after medical needs. Barbers gave free haircuts. Still other volunteers helped organize the massive outpouring of donations coming in by the hour.

Hinch, accompanied by outfielder Josh Reddick and pitcher Joe Musgrove, were among 16 Astros who dropped by on Friday. They talked about the Astros and posed for selfies with folks who'd lost their homes and most everything they had. Hinch confessed to feeling a bit self-conscious talking about baseball with people who had no idea how and when they were going to pull their lives back together.

Orbit, the floppy green Astros mascot, played with kids. Altuve strolled through the building and even danced with a star-struck evacuee. Musgrove had a pair of white spikes with him and got kids to sign them, then wore them for Saturday's doubleheader. "Look for 'em on TV," he urged.

Earlier that morning, Musgrove and relief pitcher Chris Devenski had driven to BBVA Compass Stadium, home of the Houston Dynamo MLS team, and helped load pallets of supplies designated for local communities. Several Mets players visited with first responders.

Justin Verlander, the newest Astro, donated $100,000 to military veterans, a gift the team matched. Astros ownership contributed $4 million, the Texas Rangers $1 million. Yu Darvish—yes, that Yu Darvish—donated $100,000. Altuve contributed $30,000 and thousands more in shoes and athletic gear through his promotional agreement with New Balance. McCullers teamed with a local animal group to find homes for displaced pets. Dallas Keuchel spent time with local police officers.

The Astros also opened the kitchens at Minute Maid and cooked 5,000 meals a day to be distributed in the community by the Salvation Army. The team bought 20,000 school-supply kits and 11,000 backpacks for Houston and outlying districts and rebuilt a Boys and Girls Club.

The team has also reached out to local Little Leagues that had lost playing fields and equipment. Twila Carter, executive director of the Astros' Foundation and the team's community relations department, said 7 of the 15 fields used by the Kingwood/Forest Cove League were under 20 feet of water during the peak of the flood surge. While inspecting the fields, local officials were stunned to see fish stuffed into the wire mesh at the top of the batting screens.

"We hope that we can provide a break from what's turned into some rough days for a lot of people," Hinch said during a press conference. "We're a baseball team. We provide entertainment, we try to make the city proud, and we wear 'Houston' across our chests, and we will represent this community very well. I hope it provides a smile or two. I hope it provides a break from what's going through these people's minds. To keep it in perspective we're a baseball team. We're going to do our part. We're going to try to help return to normalcy and a normal weekend in September has a lot of Astros baseball involved."

On Saturday afternoon, with thousands of Houstonians in shelters at the GRB and elsewhere, with thousands more caught up in the tedious and heartbreaking process of hauling smelly, water-logged furniture, clothes, Sheetrock, carpeting, and precious family mementoes out to the curb, it was time for baseball in Houston.

Mayor Turner, wearing an orange Astros jersey, threw out the first ball. Standing near second base, Hinch, the Astros' third-year manager spoke to the fans: "Hello, Houston. It's good to be home. We wear this [HOUSTON STRONG] patch the rest of the year to represent you. Stay strong. Be strong. And enjoy the rest of the year."

Jason Garcia was in the stands. The 32-year-old restaurant manager and lifelong Houstonian had spent a night at the GRB earlier in the week after being airlifted by Coast Guard helicopter from his home on the northeast side of the city. On Saturday, he got a haircut, worked out, and bought a ticket to the game.

"You try to get back to normal as soon as possible," he told Robert Klemko of *Sports Illustrated*. "People just need something to cheer for."

In Pearland, the Dean family, Jim and Jennifer and their kids, were watching on TV. Inside their gutted-out home, they sat on camp chairs planted on the bare concrete floor.

"To be able to watch baseball kept us normal," Jim Dean recalled weeks later. "With the Astros, we had something to look forward to, something to get lost in for a moment. I would be excited to have something to focus on that wasn't about the destruction we had gone through. Watching the game was an escape from the terrible aftermath."

"Houston was feeling a lot like a community instead of a big city," Jennifer Dean said. The city was struggling to recover and get its mojo back."

"The Astros stepped it up and they took our pride and elevated it," her husband added. "We felt like we got knocked down as a community. We needed something to get past that."

Before an announced crowd of 30,319 at Minute Maid— probably half that number were in the stands, but they were raucous—the Astros jumped on the Mets early. They put up seven runs in the first two innings against the Mets' starting pitcher— his name was Matt HARVEY, by the way—and pounded out 17 hits in route to a 12–8 victory before a crowd that included relief workers, first responders, and evacuees. The Astros' 1-2-3 hitters didn't make an out until their fourth time through the order.

The Astros won the second game, 4–1. Springer went 3-for-4 and Brad Peacock went five and a third innings, giving up just one run. Musgrove, during two and a third innings of two-hit relief work, wore those white shoes he had young evacuees autograph at the GRB.

"We felt like we were carrying everybody in our hearts," Musgrove said afterward. "Having the shoes on my feet is a constant reminder of what some people are going through and how fortunate we are." (Musgrove would be traded to Pittsburgh after the season.)

After Springer hit a two-run homer in the opener, he tapped a patch on his chest as he rounded the bases. It read: HOUSTON STRONG. The two words, reminiscent of "BOSTON STRONG" after the 2013 marathon bombing, became the team's motto, and the city's. The words alluded to all those people who wouldn't allow their lives to be washed away by a 500-year flood, who piloted tiny boats in deadly waters to rescue their neighbors, who volunteered for days at a time in community shelters to keep strangers clothed and fed. They were HOUSTON STRONG.

"The fact that they came out today to support us, it's crazy," Springer told reporters afterward. "There's thousands of people that don't have homes, they don't have belongings, and they're rallying around us. It's our job as the sports team here to do anything we can."

Asked Saturday how he planned to get his players to put aside their city's needs and focus on the job at hand, Hinch had a quick answer, one that revealed he was a different kind of baseball man: "You know what? I don't want it out of their minds. I want them to think about it this week. I want them to think about it next week. I want them to think about it next month, in six months....Obviously for these three hours—we're pros. We'll be able to compete. The baseball will take care of itself. But to be honest, I want our guys to stay connected to the rebuild."

Hinch was well aware that several Astros had more than just Harvey and the Houston flood to worry about. Carlos Beltrán, Carlos Correa, catcher Juan Centeno, and bench coach Alex Cora were all from Puerto Rico, and the massive devastation inflicted on the island by Hurricane Maria was of deep concern.

Beltrán told reporters he couldn't sleep for about 10 days. He said he did not hear from his family there for a week, until his brother relayed stories about waiting in gas lines for nearly 24 hours and his baseball academy taking on three feet of water.

"What do you need?" asked Astros owner Crane, who also happened to be a shipping magnate. "A plane," Beltrán said.

Crane chartered three planes to take 240,000 pounds of supplies down and bring people back. Beltrán announced the trip on his personal Facebook page and soon filled the return flights—his family, Dodgers utilityman Enrique Hernández's family, Indians shortstop Francisco Lindor's family. Beltrán also called around to hospitals and coordinated transportation to the mainland for cancer patients who needed to continue their treatments.

He used the money his foundation raised—$1.3 million plus the $1 million he donated personally—to buy food and water. As the death toll rose to an estimated 1,000 or more and as much of the devastated island remained without power, he tried to publicize his work, hoping to remind his fellow Americans that their countrymen in Puerto Rico still need their help.

"Right now, I'm trying to delegate a lot to my wife," he told reporters. "She told me I was going crazy, and she said, 'Carlos, you need to focus on baseball and you have to make sure other people take care of this.' But I always have a hard time when your family wants to do something."

Despite the competing concerns, the Astros continued to play great baseball, with a record of 30–14 the first three weeks in September, including an 18–3 record at Minute Maid Park. On

September 18, on a Sunday afternoon at Minute Maid, the Astros clinched a division title before 34,000 delirious fans. In their 149th game of the season, a 7–1 victory against the Mariners, the Astros' won their seventh division championship, their first in the American League West. They became the first team to win titles in three different leagues, having won two in the National League West and four in the National League Central Division before moving to the American League in 2013.

The Astros (91–58) won their division with their newest ace on the mound, the recently acquired Verlander. The former MVP and Cy Young Award winner held the Mariners to one run in seven innings, striking out 10 and walking only one. In his three starts with the Astros, all wins, Verlander's ERA was an incredible .086.

Correa, Gonzalez, and Derek Fisher each hit two-run homers. Springer blasted a solo home run. The Astros outhit the Mariners, 12–3.

A month later they were in the World Series.

CHAPTER 8

Astros Win at Home

ASTROS LEAD SERIES, 2–1

There's no place like home.

DOROTHY GALE, KANSAS STORM SURVIVOR

O n a joyous Friday evening in Houston, the temperature more suited to a Fall Classic, Astros fans were lining up hours before game time to get into Minute Maid Park. Like the players they came to support, the fans were a good-natured bunch, most of them wearing their orange Astros gear, a few in the throwback rainbow jerseys. Shuffling toward the green wrought-iron gates, they chatted with strangers about the team's chances, about the pitching matchups, about José Altuve's MVP chances.

They liked these guys, and not only because they're winning. Whether the fans filing into Minute Maid knew it, the Astros' vaunted analytics department had helped craft not only an exceptional team but also an exceptional culture.

John Eliot, an associate professor of sport management at Texas A&M University who researches the behavioral and brain science of athletes, put it this way in an interview with Houston's

ABC affiliate: "What the Astros are doing is that stuff that creates winning. If you've got a great culture and you're focused on day-to-day executing, that culture, the guys, the locker room, they go there not to win a ball game but to help each other play great and to play great baseball. That's one step removed from winning."

Manager A. J. Hinch, in a post-Series guest appearance at a Houston eatery called Pluckers Wing Bar, made a similar point: "The clubhouse was very much like a group of best friends. There were team dinners on the road organized by [Carlos] Beltrán and others. You were expected to go—sometimes 40 guys—and the host picks up the tab."

There were a few fights, he said, "but brothers have fights too. But the team was integrated, not just outfielders hanging out with outfielders, for example. People like Altuve, [Lance] McCullers—they're great connectors. It was just a culture of trying to help each other."

————————

To throw out the ceremonial first ball for the first World Series game played in the Bayou City since 2005, the Astros tapped another great connector, arguably the most popular athlete in town (with the exception, perhaps, of Altuve), Houston's celebrity answer to Hoffman, Seinfeld, Timberlake, and friends. J. J. Watt, the Houston Texans' three-time Defensive Player of the Year, slowly made his way to the mound on crutches, his left leg in a black cast after breaking it in week five of the NFL season.

Watt had visited the Astros clubhouse a couple of times during the season, was friends with a lot of the guys on the team, and was a vocal cheerleader on Twitter. The Astros admired him as much as the rest of Houston did, not only because of his stellar performance on the field but also because of his ties to the community.

When Altuve sent each of his teammates a bottle of Crown Royal after the World Series, he sent one to Watt as well. The Texans star is "absolutely a part of the squad," he said.

"I love J. J.," Hinch told reporters before Game 3. "He's such a pillar of our community, and part of the city in so many ways. And really defines kind of the fabric of this city. And what he's done through his hurricane efforts, recovery efforts, is nothing short of extraordinary."

It was Watt's first public appearance since the injury, and Houston fans greeted him with a sustained standing ovation. Like Hinch, they knew the story of how the Wisconsin native desperately wanted to do something to help his adopted city as he was forced to the sidelines for the rest of the Texans season.

"That's our city," Watt had said in a video he shared on social media as he watched helplessly from a hotel on the road as Harvey swamped Houston. He hit on the idea of raising maybe $200,000 for local hurricane relief efforts. To Watt's shock and happy surprise, the final figure turned out to be nearly $36 million.

The personable, young giant wore a Astros cap backward and an orange Astros jersey and was accompanied by his soccer-player girlfriend, Kealia Ohai of the Houston Dash. He handed his right crutch to Ohai to hold before he delivered a pitch to Astros pitcher Dallas Keuchel. Throwing with a crutch under his left arm and unable to take a step while he threw, Watt's toss made it to Keuchel on the fly but was wide of the plate, unlike most deliveries from the pinpoint-precise Keuchel himself. The Astros' bearded ace signed the ball and greeted Watt with a hug.

———————

For the Astros and their screaming, standing fans crammed into Minute Maid, the best description of Game 3 would be two words: Peacock Proud. Brad Peacock, a starter turned reliever, pitched three and two-thirds innings in relief, retired 11 of 12 batters on 53 pitches, and didn't allow a hit. His save was the first of a career dating back to 2011. All this, the *Houston Chronicle*'s Jake Kaplan noted, from "an unassuming 29-year-old right-hander so unsure of his status with the Astros that before spring training he warned his wife they might have to move to Japan."

"The season has meant a lot," Peacock told reporters after the game. "I've said it before many times, I don't think I was going to make the team in spring training. And someone got hurt and I just had a save in the World Series. It's unbelievable, man. I'm never going to forget this, ever."

As it turned out, Peacock didn't have to travel to the Far East to compete against a pitcher from Japan. Yu Darvish, a six-foot-five-inch right-hander of Japanese-Iranian heritage, had tamed the Arizona Diamondbacks and the Chicago Cubs in his previous post-season starts. He had allowed just four runs (three earned) in 30⅔ innings over five starts, with a 35–2 strikeout-to-walk ratio. His only two runs allowed in 11⅓ postseason innings were solo homers.

The Astros knew him well from his time with the Texas Rangers. He was 4–1 with a 2.16 ERA at Minute Maid since 2013. That was the year he was one out away from a perfect game at the Houston ballpark.

"He's got 15 pitches you have to deal with, from different angles, and he can reach back and have velocity," Hinch said before the game. "But if you can get him in the strike zone, like any pitcher in the Big Leagues, we've done damage to every good pitcher in the strike zone. When we expand, it's tough."

Darvish gave up a leadoff double to George Springer in an 18-pitch first inning. As Springer noted after the game, Darvish wasn't able to entice hitters to go after off-the-plate pitches, the key to his success over the years.

Falling behind 2–1 to Yuli Gurriel, leading off the second, the Dodger right-hander delivered a 94.6-mile-per-hour sinker that didn't. It was up in the strike zone—the better for Gurriel to see—and the 33-year-old rookie from Cuba lined it to the left for a 379-foot homer into the Crawford Boxes, the bleachers in left field. Minute Maid's 17-year veteran train conductor Bobby Vasquez—aka Bobby Dynamite—powered up the old-fashioned locomotive, its coal tinder filled with what appeared to be basketball-sized oranges. On its track 90 feet above the left field wall, the train made its World Series debut, its piercing whistle barely audible above the roar of a crowd gone crazy.

Unfortunately, just for a second, an ebullient Gurriel went crazy too. Back in the dugout after his triumphant home-run trot around the bases, laughing with his teammates, TV cameras caught him lifting the skin of his eyes and appearing to mouth the Spanish word *Chinito,* an insult that translates "little Chinese boy." Most players on both teams missed it, but social media didn't. Twitter erupted. The ensuing uproar would play out the next day, with

Gurriel telling teammates later that he was trying to communicate that he had always been lucky hitting against Japanese pitchers—he played a year in Japan—and that he meant no disrespect.

Meanwhile, Gurriel's teammates were disrespecting the hell out of the sliders and fastballs Darvish was serving up. Josh Reddick, the fiery left fielder who had been quiet for most of the series, doubled down the left field line. Evan Gattis, the husky designated hitter, walked on seven pitches, prompting Dodger manager Dave Roberts to stroll to the mound and try to calm his struggling starter.

Whatever Roberts said didn't help. Marwin Gonzalez's long single off the left-center field wall scored Reddick, and Brian McCann singled home Gattis. After Springer lined out to second base—the first out of the inning, on Darvish's 28th pitch—Alex Bregman brought Gonzalez home with a sacrifice fly for a 4–0 lead. When Altuve lined a double off the left-center field wall, manager Roberts had seen enough. He called on reliever Kenta Maeda, who needed two pitches to retire Carlos Correa on a fly ball.

A few weeks after the season, an anonymous Astros player suggested to *Sports Illustrated* that Astros hitters knew what was coming. Darvish was tipping his pitches. Nobody connected to either team confirmed the rumor, but it seemed there was something to it, as Roberts intimated to the *Los Angeles Times*. "We had conversations about that with Yu, trying to kind of pin it down," the manager said. "Obviously, we weren't successful. I think that there's something to that, but there's also a lot more, for me, to execution."

Whatever the reason for the Astros' explosion, Minute Maid Park was in a state of towel-waving fan frenzy. The players had told Hinch before the game they wanted the stadium roof closed, regardless of the weather. The Dodgers, their ears ringing at that moment, could understand why. The Minute Maid roof was a strategic factor, the way Fenway Park's Green Monster has been over the years.

"You know, it gets loud. It gets real loud," pitcher Charlie Morton explained. "But for me that's awesome, because it feels like the whole city is behind me. It kind of envelops you into that moment. And in a lot of ways you can get lost in a good way. You can kind of let some things go and just compete. So it allows you to be emotional in a good way."

"It's quite an environment," Hinch said. "When we play under the roof, our fans get going....It's a great environment at home. I think that's what makes people feel good."

The 4–0 lead reminded all those standing, yelling, towel-waving fans that these were the Astros they had enjoyed all year, a team that pounded and pounded and pounded their opponents into submission. Now the question would be, What about the pitching?

The man on the mound was 24-year-old McCullers, the pitcher who, in the aftermath of the hurricane, had railed at the Texans unwillingness to swap series with the Astros. Hinch had described his young pitcher as "a confident kid. He believes in his best stuff matched up against the best stuff of the other guy, that he's going to be better. He's a challenge-first type guy....He's able to keep his emotions in check. His demeanor is very good. He's got just enough cockiness to him that is attractive as a competitor.

"And he wants the ball. He wants to finish. If you ask him, 'What are you going to do tomorrow?' he's going to say, 'I'm going to throw nine scoreless.' And he believes it. And he thinks it's my fault if it doesn't happen because I took him out."

The hard-throwing right-hander, son of a major leaguer nicknamed Baby Goose (for retired reliever Richard "Goose" Gossage), had been superb before the All-Star break, but after suffering a back injury, he wasn't quite his old self when he returned. Friday night was his second start of the postseason and his fourth appearance. He had looked good in Game 4 of the American League Championship Series, with a six-inning, one-run start against the Yankees, and he had pitched four shutout innings in relief in Game 7.

McCullers had no problems the first two innings against the Dodgers, needing just 25 pitches and allowing only a two-out single to Logan Forsythe. The Dodgers caught up with him in the third.

Maybe his back stiffened during the 30-minute break on the bench, happily watching his teammates pound Darvish. Back on the mound, he lost sight of the plate, walking the bases loaded on 19 pitches.

"You want to make a pitching coach crazy? Get handed a 4–0 lead and then go to the mound and walk the No. 8, No. 9 and No. 1 hitters to load the bases with nobody out. That's what Lance McCullers Jr. just did," Dave Waldstein observed on the *New York Times* blog.

It could have been worse for the hometown boys. Up came young Corey Seager, who had hit a two-run homer off Justin Verlander in Game 2. This time, on a 1–1 count, Seager hit a hard grounder to Gurriel, whose throw to second set in motion a picture-perfect 3-6-1 double play, with McCullers's foot barely skimming the bag in time. Joc Pederson scored on the play, but McCullers avoided additional damage by getting Justin Turner to ground out.

McCullers was like a man on a high wire during the next couple of innings, like Philippe Petit constantly flirting with disaster. With one out, Yasiel Puig hit a line drive that deflected off third baseman Bregman's glove and into foul territory. Racing to first, Puig didn't see that the ball had pinballed around between the bag and the angled wall and that Bregman had not made a throw. When he realized the ball was still on the ground, he got a late start heading to second and was thrown out on a close play.

With one out in the fifth, Pederson doubled, then took third on a groundout. Taylor lined a pitch to center field, but Springer's diving catch saved a run. The Astros picked up another run in the bottom of the inning, thanks to a couple of singles and a throwing error by reliever Tony Watson.

McCullers ran out of juice in the sixth. He walked Seager and gave up a double to Turner. He managed to strike out Cody Bellinger—running the National League Rookie of the Year's World Series futility to 0-for-10 with six strikeouts—but with Puig coming up, manager Hinch figured his starter had gone far enough. McCullers handed off to Peacock.

Astros analytics told Hinch that Peacock's four-seam fastball, up in the zone, matched up well with the Dodgers lineup, although it took him a few pitches to settle in. He got a soft groundout from Puig, which sent Seager home. With two outs he threw a wild pitch to pinch hitter Chase Utley that allowed Turner to score. Utley ended up popping out in foul territory to end the inning, but the Dodgers must have felt better with the score 5–3.

Both teams were scoreless in the seventh, as Peacock avoided any problems with a two-out walk. In the bottom of the inning, manager Roberts pushed the button on his reliever assembly line. Gurriel smashed a hard double off Brandon Morrow, and Reddick, noticing the infield playing deep, tried to bunt him over but popped up to first baseman Bellinger for the first out. Tony Cingrani got the second out—between an intentional walk and a single—but was pulled with the bases loaded. With Ross Stripling on the mound, Springer pounded a fly ball to deep center field, which got the crowd excited before the ball landed in center fielder Chris Taylor's glove.

On to the eighth, and Peacock, who started for the Astros in the AL Division Series before McCullers replaced him in the rotation in the ALCS, continued to dominate. The right-hander pitched a third consecutive scoreless inning, striking out Seager, getting Turner to pop out to the catcher, and ending it with yet another strikeout of Bellinger, the rookie's fourth strikeout in four at bats. The youngster hardly resembled the guy who had hit 39 home runs during the regular season, a National League record for a rookie.

Catcher McCann, a 13-year MLB veteran beloved by his pitchers, helped keep Peacock focused. "I've never seen a World Series–caliber team that doesn't have a stable catcher," Hinch said. "Doesn't have to be the most notable guy. There's been catchers that aren't the biggest names. But just stability behind that. And Brian really does embody that type of characteristic.

"So we need him at times like this, where there's so much pressure. So much anxiety that goes into every single pitch. He's been spectacular with how he's managed the games and controlled our pitching staffs and been locked in behind the plate. And that's that veteran leadership that we don't know how to quantify, we don't know how to measure, but we do know when we have it."

McCann said after the game that Peacock rarely used his money pitch, a slider. McCann said he kept calling for the fastball, and Peacock went with his catcher's judgment and experience.

"It was exploding on them," McCann told the *Chronicle*'s Kaplan, talking about Peacock's fastball. "He's got one of the better fastballs in the game, too. He's got one of those, like balls that ride on the same plane. He's got a two-seamer and a four-seamer, so it's kind of two different pitches in one. The hitters tell you a lot from their reactions, and we just kept going with it."

Waldstein, the *New York Times* reporter, was impressed. "I've been expounding a lot on the Dodgers bullpen situation," he observed, "and meanwhile Brad Peacock has thrown 2⅔ scoreless innings and is really doing some important work out of the Houston bullpen. What else would you expect from a guy who went 13–2 in the regular season? Well, the Yankees and Red Sox knocked him around pretty hard in the previous two rounds of the playoffs, but his stuff has been effective against the Dodgers."

After the game, Peacock told reporters that Hinch had asked him if he felt good when he got to the dugout after the eighth. "I said, 'yeah.'"

"All right. You're going back out," Hinch told him.

"I'm shocked," Peacock recalled. "I'm just glad he gave me the opportunity to do that. And it was a lot of fun out there, for sure."

Peacock walked back out to the mound to start the ninth, in part because Hinch and pitching coach Brent Strom had noticed that he was still keeping his wrist directly behind the ball on release, a sign that he wasn't tiring. Hinch, who's allowed two computers in the dugout to help him with the analytics, was going with his gut on this one. As owner Jim Crane put it, "A. J. believes you have to manage on the field, at that moment."

Fans could feel it in the air. Minute Maid was loud, so loud, in fact, that you couldn't hear the person sitting—or more likely standing—next to you. The Astros were three outs away from a 2–1 lead in the Series.

Astros fans had no reason to worry. Peacock's fun continued. He got Puig to flail at strike three, Utley to ground out on a dribbler to the mound, and Yasmani Grandal to fly out.

Game over. The Astros were 7–0 at Minute Maid.

The Astros had won a World Series game at home. Craig Biggio, on hand for the victory, was beaming. So was Jeff Bagwell. Nolan Ryan. Mike Scott. Jim Wynn. Rusty Staub. All those Astros from years gone by, several of whom had come close, might have pounded an old glove they had around the house, maybe swung an imaginary bat. Certainly they raised a glass. Astros who had worn the rainbow jerseys, Astros who barely remembered seeing them—they all had reason to cheer.

As waves of happy fans surged into downtown, blocking traffic around Minute Maid, Peacock was in the clubhouse talking to reporters. "It's unbelievable, man," he said. "I'm never going to forget this, ever."

CHAPTER 9

Dodgers Spoil Astros' Saturday Night

SERIES TIED, 2-2

No one is perfect. That includes both you and I.

DODGERS PITCHER YU DARVISH

RESPONDING TO YULI GURREIL'S INSULTING GESTURE

On Saturday morning, Major League Baseball Commissioner Rob Manfred handed down Yuli Gurriel's sentence. The Astros first baseman would be suspended for five games at the start of the 2018 regular season, punishment for the racially offensive gesture he had made the night before, after his home run off Japanese-born Yu Darvish. Gurriel would see his salary shrink during the suspension, $322,581 out of $12 million annually. The Astros said they'd donate the money to charity. MLB said that Gurriel would be taking sensitivity training during the off-season.

Earlier in the week, before the incident, A. J. Hinch had described Gurriel's role on the team in rosy terms. "Having to learn a new country, having to learn a new team, a new position, he's been remarkable," Hinch said. "He's a funny guy behind the scenes. He's very under control. The moment's never too big. And to be honest with you, of all of our players in the postseason, he's been the calmest and the most like himself during this run."

Now Gurriel had embarrassed the organization and blemished a feel-good World Series, and he seemed to know it. He also seemed to realize he was lucky. The hard-hitting first baseman could have been suspended during the Series, but at a pregame news conference Manfred explained his reasoning for postponing the punishment.

"First of all, I felt it was important that the suspension carried with it the penalty of lost salary," Manfred said. "Secondly, I felt it was unfair to punish the other 24 players on the Astros' roster. I wanted the burden of this discipline to fall primarily on the wrongdoer.

"Third, I was impressed in my conversation with Yu Darvish by his desire to move forward, and I felt that moving this suspension to the beginning of the season would help in that regard. Last, when I originally began thinking about the discipline, I thought that delaying the suspension would allow the player the opportunity to exercise his rights under the grievance procedure."

Immediately after the game Friday night, Darvish said, through an interpreter: "Of course, Houston has Asian fans and Japanese fans. Acting like that is disrespectful to people around the world and the Houston organization."

Later, in a tweet, he wrote, "No one is perfect. That includes both you and I. What he [did] today isn't right, but I believe we should put our effort into learning rather than to accuse him. If we can take something from this, this is a giant step for mankind."

Manfred met with Gurriel, who expressed remorse and assured the commissioner he would offer a private apology to Darvish.

"During last night's game, I made an offensive gesture that was indefensible," Gurriel said in a prepared statement released by the Astros. "I sincerely apologize to everyone that I offended with my actions. I deeply regret it. I would particularly like to apologize to Yu Darvish, a pitcher that I admire and respect. I would also like to apologize to the Dodgers organization, the Astros, Major League Baseball, and to all fans across the game."

Reporters asked Astros pitcher Dallas Keuchel afterward whether the Gurriel incident had been a distraction.

Keuchel offered a diplomatic answer. "I don't think so," he said. "It would be a distraction, I would say, if he was a guy that was so flamboyant and always making trouble off the field or on the field, and that's not Yuli."

Before Game 1 in Los Angeles, an 89-year-old former pitcher for the old Brooklyn Dodgers had thrown out the ceremonial first pitch. Fans of a certain age knew who he was. His name was Don Newcombe. He was African American and he had signed with the Dodgers two years after his teammate Jackie Robinson had burst through Major League Baseball's color line. For Robinson, for Newcombe, and for the Cleveland Indians' Larry Doby, the American League's first black player, vicious racial slurs, insults, and blatant discrimination, both on and off the field, were commonplace. These baseball pioneers even endured death threats. That Gurriel's offense was relatively minor, that it was handled with dispatch by Major League Baseball, and that Gurriel seemed genuinely apologetic would seem to be a measure of progress exactly 70 seasons after Robinson broke through.

Still, the thoughtless gesture was bigger than it seemed.

On Saturday a *Los Angeles Times* reporter talked to Britny Cuellar, who was walking along the sidewalk with her husband outside Minute Maid Park, pushing their two-year-old daughter in a stroller. The Gurriel gesture caused them to groan, Cuellar said, because they worried it would overshadow everything the team had accomplished and all that the city had been through since Harvey.

"I just think he was being childish," she said of Gurriel. "I don't think he meant any harm from it."

Cuellar, a 27-year-old elementary school teacher of Mexican descent, told the *Times* she thought Houston would view the incident differently from the way it was being reported in the media, because its residents were comfortable with the city's diversity. She said she was proud to see how the city came together after Hurricane Harvey, noting that Islamic centers opened their doors to flood victims and that people of all races did everything they could to help.

Houston, the nation's most diverse city, is home to a massive Asian population, so large, in fact, that neighborhoods on the city's west side have street signs in Vietnamese. The city's Asian restaurants rank among the finest in the country. As Cuellar emphasized, it's a city comfortable with its Benetton mix of colors, customs, and nationalities.

"You go to the games," she said, "and you see everybody different here. Black, white, Hispanic, Indian, Asian."

Football writer Spencer Hall was more expansive about the city's sprawling diversity. "It's sprawling in more than one sense of the word," he wrote. "Houston can be super-Texas-country: the requisite pickup trucks, gun shops (oh my god the gun shops), churches, the giant lawns in all the easy marks. There's also the biggest Hindu temple I've seen outside of India because of a booming South Asian population and a slew of Spanish-language radio presets in the rental car thanks to a huge Hispanic community. The banh mi game is extremely real, thanks to the Vietnamese and other immigrants who settled in Harris County after 1975. The Chinese community is large enough that you can fly EVA Air direct to IAH from Taipei. One in four Houstonians is foreign-born, including the University of Houston's President, Renu Khator, who hails from India."

Gurriel's racially insensitive gesture was also out of character for a team as diverse and welcoming as its city, a team whose youthful exuberance had won the hearts of fans, among Houstonians initially and then baseball fans everywhere. Although Gurriel at 33 was slightly older than the Astros' better-known stars, his yellow hair standing straight up like an unruly shock of wheat—his teammates liked to ruffle it for good luck—and his playfulness in the clubhouse made him one of the gang.

"If you polled our guys and asked who's the nicest guy on the team, 40 guys on a 40-man roster, they'd say it's Yuli," Alex Bregman said on a radio show weeks later. "He's the best teammate I ever had." (Bregman, by the way, takes lessons to perfect his New Mexican–accented *español* to better communicate with his infield mates, all three Latin American.)

Astros fans knew their stories, including Gurriel's. Born Yulieski Gurriel in Sancti Spiritus, Cuba, he came from a distinguished baseball family. His father was known as "the Babe Ruth" of Cuba, and his younger brother, Lourdes Gurriel, had signed with the Toronto Blue Jays.

Yuli was the best player on the island when he and his brother defected in 2016 after playing in a tournament in the Dominican Republic. He eventually signed a five-year, $47.5 million contract with the Astros. He brought a big personality to the clubhouse, but Hinch prized him for his steadiness on the field. He was a rookie, but he'd been playing the game a long time. And he had made a serious mistake.

———————————

The man playing next to Gurriel on the Astros' United Nations infield, a leadoff man turned slugger, was arguably the team's biggest favorite.

Keuchel tells a story about encountering José Altuve when both were playing minor league ball. Riding a bus to a game, he kept hearing a voice from the back, a voice he couldn't place, speaking in loud rapid-fire Spanish. Whoever it was, he sounded like he hadn't hit puberty yet, Keuchel recalled, laughing. "He sounded like he shouldn't even be playing baseball."

It didn't take long for Keuchel to realize that the Latino guy with the little kid's voice was a ballplayer. "I knew there was no doubt that he was going to be a star at some point," he said. "I didn't know that he was going to actually be this good....I couldn't be happier for the guy, because he is an all-American dude."

Actually an all-Americas dude. Astros fans know the story about their five-foot-six-inch MVP—he's really five-five—from

Maracay, Venezuela, a city of just over a million people between the mountains and Lake Valencia. They know he grew up playing baseball day and night, that he was always told he was too small. They know that when he was 16 in 2006 he attended an Astros try-out camp. At the end of the first day he waited to hear his name called among those the Astros wanted to talk to about signing a contract. Waiting and waiting and not hearing "Altuve," he took his glove and spikes and trudged home.

Seven other teams also had passed on the little second baseman. "Coming to us was his last shot," Al Pedrique, an Astros special assistant, told Hunter Atkins of the *Houston Chronicle*. Pedrique, a former big league infielder, couldn't get over how Altuve handled himself, how fast he was, how quick his hands were.

"His hand-eye coordination is so much better than most people, he's abnormal," Astros broadcaster Steve Sparks, a former major league pitcher, told me. (That's a compliment born of awe.)

Sparks has a theory about Altuve's hand-eye prowess: hitting bottle caps with a broomstick for hours every day when he was a kid. (Sparks's theory makes sense, although it doesn't guarantee a major league future for everybody. Growing up in Central Texas, I hit rocks with a broomstick for hours at a time on long, hot summer days. "Homers" over our back fence landed in Mr. Lee's adjacent chicken yard. Unlike the incredible Altuve, I didn't end up in the majors, perhaps because Mr. Lee complained to my dad that his hens, bombarded from above, had stopped laying. I had to retire my broomstick early.)

Despite Pedrique's sparkling assessment, the Astros sent Altuve home. The disappointed teenager assumed the decision was final, but his father, Carlos, insisted that he go back the next day. And so he did.

A few of the scouts gave him a second look that second day and saw something that computers and analytics don't always pick up. He had baseball instincts, baseball intelligence. He worked hard. He was determined to get better. He simply refused to allow his stature to dictate his dream. The Astros offered the littlest guy on the field, the guy his pals called "Gigante," a contract that was anything but. He signed for $15,000.

Through five seasons in the minor leagues, Altuve was a fine hitter, posting a .327 batting average and an .867 on-base plus slugging percentage. And yet, nobody paid much attention, even when he made it to the majors. As Alex Putterman, writing in the *Atlantic,* put it, "he was regularly written off as a role player at best or a fluke at worst."

That perception began to change in 2014, Altuve's third full season with the Astros. The little guy who wears his pants knickers-style, right at the knees, suddenly blossomed into one of the best hitters in baseball, known for his keen eye and dazzling bat speed. He learned to lay off pitches he couldn't hit and won his first Silver Slugger award. Adding to his offensive repertoire, he made himself an accomplished base stealer.

Something even more incredible happened the next year, in 2015. He started powering the ball over the fence—15 home runs in 2015, 24 in '16, 24 in '17. Arguably the strongest guy on the team and probably the fastest, he had developed into one of the most formidable hitters in baseball.

Reporters prior to the first game in LA asked manager Hinch what Altuve meant to the ball club.

"Well, I don't know any more ways to describe José other than he's as close to perfect as you can imagine as a manager," he said. "He does everything right. And I've used this before, but he's every bit what's right about our team and our organization and represents so much of what we do."

Hinch raved about his consistency. "From April to May through June, July, August into September and now we're seeing October, I don't know anybody that's been able to maintain their performance and improve their performance over time than him," the Astros manager said.

"So we're hard to beat when he's right, and he's right a lot of days," Hinch added. "The hits are real. The defense is real. The presence that he's starting to grow into as a leader, albeit a quiet one, is felt by all of us, whether it's players, coaches, organization, and the whole city of Houston."

Altuve and his double-play partner, shortstop Carlos Correa, choreographed a celebratory ritual whenever one or the other crossed home plate. Delighted fans got used to seeing Correa leap out of the dugout, arms waving, like a little kid on Christmas morning and—if it's Altuve who has scored—skip toward his teammate. Halfway between the dugout and home plate, both men meet and leap, their arms held high like courting pelicans, big grins on their faces. Their silly, little ritual had become a trademark.

Larry Dierker, a former Astros pitcher and later manager, told Astros TV announcer Bill Brown that all the celebrating—Altuve and Correa, as well as their teammates—gave him pause initially. It mocked baseball's button-down tradition, compared to other sports. But then he changed his mind.

"I thought, you know, if I was a pitching I wouldn't appreci-ate that. Somebody might go down," he told Brown. "But the other teams don't seem to object to it in this day and age, so maybe it's OK. The more I saw the team, the more I liked it, and I began to change the way I saw the team. It's not like football—'watch me,' as they dance in the end zone after a touchdown—because they weren't trying to get attention for themselves. Almost everything they did, they were celebrating the other guy and not themselves."

They were boys having fun, young guys reveling in their suc-cess, and yet there was more to the relationship than youth-ful exuberance, *Houston Chronicle* photographer Karen Warren noticed on the first day of spring training, 2016. She happened to see Altuve and Correa sauntering out to the practice field, caps on backward, enjoying each other's company in the Florida sun-shine. The two guys stepped across the foul line onto the playing field itself, and Altuve reached up—he's always reaching up—and turned Correa's cap around. The small gesture was a reminder from the veteran to the second-year man that they were profes-sionals, that it was time to get down to business.

Correa, who was evolving into the unofficial captain of the infield during the championship run, idolizes Altuve. Their lockers are side by side, and they spend a lot of time together off the field.

Altuve's teammates were in awe of his abilities, or, to be more precise, his ability to consistently improve. "Honestly, I never seen anything like him," the veteran Carlos Beltrán told reporters during the American League Championship Series. "He does a lot of things in the batting cage that sometimes you would not want a lot of guys to do it. He hit across, he pull the outside pitch, and shoot it down the line. Normally you would tell a guy like him, 'Man, go with the pitch. Make sure you stride toward the pitcher.'

"He's a unique hitter. He does spend a lot of work, a lot of time in the media room watching pitchers, working on his swing. He take a lot of pride into hitting, even though he's real humble about it, which is great for me to see that in a guy that has won three batting championship. It's amazing."

There was more about the remarkable young man from Venezuela. "What I thought about is how this guy represents the city of Houston as well as anyone," said former Yankee great Alex Rodriguez, an analyst during the World Series for the Fox Network. "Here is a guy who has the heart of a lion. You can measure his size, but you can't measure what he represents, his character, and how genuine he is."

Altuve, because of his size, has had to fight for everything he's achieved; Correa, big, fast, strong, and gifted, would seem to have it all from the beginning. He would dispute that, and so would his family.

Ben Reiter of *Sports Illustrated* wrote that Correa's father, Carlos Sr., was nicknamed 24/7 in the Correas' hometown of Santa Isabel, a relatively small town on Puerto Rico's southern coast. He worked constantly—a construction job beginning at 4:30 in the morning, a maintenance job for the town's parks and recreation department for several hours in the middle of the day, and another construction shift in the evening.

Friends and neighbors had another nickname for the elder Correa after work: Hitler. That's what they called him for the relentless way he drove his talented son on the baseball field. From 8:30 until 10:30 every evening—six days a week, sometimes seven—starting when his son was in elementary school, Carlos Sr. took him to a field near the house and hit grounders to him or threw batting practice.

Neighbors driving by shouted at the older man through their car windows. "They would be like, 'That's too much for a little kid!'" Carlos Jr. told Reiter. "Seven years old, eight years old, I'm taking hundreds of grounders and hundreds of swings."

Correa's father pushed him, for sure, but the youngster wanted to be out there. According to Jeff Luhnow, the Astros' general manager, that same work ethic, that drive, is still an integral part of the young shortstop's makeup.

―――――――――

When the boys of a storm-tossed summer trotted onto the field Saturday night, they were determined to end the Series in Houston. Two more wins; that's all they needed. With seven wins and zero losses at home during the postseason, it certainly seemed possible.

On the mound for the Astros was Charlie Morton, 34, a veteran who had never lived up to his potential during an injury-riddled career, although the Astros hoped his stellar outing in their Game 7 win in the ALCS was a portent.

"Because he's so genuine and quiet and unassuming," Hinch had said, speaking of Morton, "there'd be days where you don't hear him at all, and he's just part of the team, that you can sometimes confuse that quietness with a lack of confidence or a lack of competitiveness, and that's not the case. This guy is confident. He wants the ball. He's competitive. Once he gets on the rubber, I think he feels like he can dictate the game. His first 96-mile-an-hour fastball will prove that."

Morton had always had good stuff, but he simply couldn't stay healthy. Still, the analytics guys saw something. They were particularly impressed with his curveball, enough so that they signed him to a two-year, $14 million contract.

He seemed to be worth every penny of that contract on Halloween night. Bedeviling the Dodgers with darting split-fingered fastballs, mixing in the occasional curveball and cutter, he allowed only three baserunners over six and a third innings. He struck out seven without issuing a walk. "You don't get much better stuff than that," Dodger starter Alex Wood said after the game.

In the sixth inning, the Dodgers had runners at first and third with one out. Third baseman Bregman glanced toward the dugout, where Astros bench coach Alex Cora pointed to his head. "Think," Cora was saying. On any ball to his left, Bregman would attempt to start an inning-ending double play. On any ball in front of him, he would throw home. He shuffled a few steps off the bag.

In that brief moment between pitches, Bregman might have been thinking about a similar situation during a September 24 game against the California Angels at Minute Maid. With runners at first and third, Bregman fielded a ground ball hit by Justin Upton and tried to turn an inning-ending double play. Upton beat the throw to first, a run scored, and the Angels won the game.

Bregman trotted to the dugout at the end of the inning and explained to Hinch and Cora what he was thinking when he threw to second. They nodded, and then Hinch offered a pithy bit of managerial wisdom in reply (as translated by Jeff Passan of Yahoo

Sports): "In the playoffs, you'd better throw that [expletive] ball home. We preserve runs in the playoffs."

Or, Bregman might have been thinking about the spectacular play he had made a week earlier on the Yankees' Greg Bird in the fifth inning of Game 7 of the ALCS, a one-run game that the Astros went on to win. On that play, Bregman made a perfect throw to the third base side of home plate, about six inches off the ground. It was the only throw he could have made that would give Brian McCann a chance to make the tag and then hang onto the ball as Bird, spikes first, slid into his left wrist.

And now it was déjà vu all over again, to quote the esteemed baseball philosopher Lawrence Peter Berra, aka Yogi (who was an Astros coach in the late 1980s). Chris Taylor bounced a chopper to the left side of the infield, Bregman charged, fielded it cleanly, and fired a strike to the plate. McCann laid an easy tag on a sliding Austin Barnes. Astros fans went wild.

"We have athletes all over the field. We do execute plays," Hinch said.

Meanwhile, Morton was pitching well, but Wood had a no-hitter going into the sixth inning. He was never in command the way his Astros counterpart was, but he did what he needed to do.

The Astros simply couldn't hit him, until George Springer stepped into the box in the sixth. Dodgers manager Dave Roberts stayed with lefty Wood, even though Springer, hitting from the right side, posted a .972 on-base slugging percentage against left-handers during the regular season.

"I thought Alex earned the opportunity—obviously, the way he was throwing the baseball, didn't give up any hard contact—to continue to go," Roberts told reporters afterward.

Wood fell behind in the count with three straight balls. He threw a fastball at the knees for a strike and then a curveball out over the plate. Springer drove it over the Crawford Boxes to give Houston the lead, 1–0.

The Dodgers chased Morton in the seventh. Cody Bellinger, who revived the Dodgers' offense when he was called up in April, had looked like he was swinging a giant celery stick throughout the Series. He had gone hitless his first 13 times up.

This time, though, he pounded a 3–2 curveball into deep left field. As the youngster coasted into second base, he lifted his hands toward the heavens, presumably thanking the baseball gods for his release from hitters' hell.

Enduring his dastardly slump, he had tried to follow the advice of teammates and coaches, who had encouraged him to simplify.

"Swing at strikes," advised Andrew Friedman, Dodgers president. "Take balls. Have fun." On the other side of the field, a similar formula had worked all season for Springer and several of his young teammates.

After Morton exited to a standing ovation in the seventh, his bullpen buddies faltered. Will Harris came on to retire Yasiel Puig on a deep fly to right field, but Logan Forsythe followed by lining a 2–0 fastball for a single that easily scored Bellinger.

The Dodgers weren't done. In the ninth, Ken Giles, who had surrendered a two-run lead in Game 2, gave up a single to Corey Seager and a walk to Justin Turner. Bellinger followed by driving a 1–0 fastball into the left-center gap for a double that scored Seager and sent Turner to third. After a sacrifice fly by Austin Barnes padded the lead, Joc Pederson hit a three-run homer to quiet the 43,322 fans at Minute Maid Park.

Giles was disgusted with himself, and after the game offered no excuses. "They were all crappy pitches, not where I wanted them," he told reporters. "I need to do better. I need to pick up this team. I need to carry my weight."

In the bottom of the ninth, Dodgers closer Kenley Jansen surrendered a solo home run to Bregman. It was only the second hit of the game for the Astros.

Cosseted by his comfortable lead, Jansen had little to worry about. As the last out settled into Taylor's glove in center field, the guys in visitors' gray and Dodger blue raced onto the field to celebrate a tough win. Under the Minute Maid roof, the orange-clad crowd looked on in silence and then began shuffling toward the exits and heading for their cars.

Houston native David Fahrenthold was making his way out of Minute Maid, but he wasn't driving. A national affairs reporter for the *Washington Post*, a 2017 Pulitzer Prize winner, and an Astros fan since he was 8 years old, he had flown in from DC to take in Game 4 with his dad. He told me that after witnessing the Astros' loss, the two were among a large crowd waiting to board Houston's light-rail line. It was the weekend before Halloween, so almost as many costume-wearing partygoers as orange-clad Astros fans were waiting on the train platform near the ballpark.

As the Fahrentholds waited, they noticed a man in a full-body chicken costume on the opposite platform bump shoulders with a fan wearing a vintage rainbow-style Astros jersey, the name Biggio stenciled on the back. The obviously inebriated fan took a swing at chicken man, who ripped off his beaked yellow mask and swung back with his wing—er, fist. The train was late because of postgame traffic and crowds, so passengers on the platform had nothing better to do but watch the two men banging away at each other.

After a few minutes, the Halloweener chickened out, briefly, and then decided he still had a bone to pick with the Astros fan. He ripped off his chicken head again and resumed the fight. "Chicken, give up!" the crowd shouted. "Chicken, it's not worth it."

The Fahrentholds called Uber.

CHAPTER 10

The Judge, the Colt .45s, the Astrodome

The Eiffel Tower is nice, but you can't play ball there.

HARRIS COUNTY JUDGE ROY HOFHEINZ

Until the wild victory in Los Angeles in Game 2, followed by the Game 3 victory in Houston, the Astros had never won a World Series game in their 56 years of existence. The Astros had been to a World Series, once, in 2005, but managed to lose four straight to the Chicago White Sox in what is probably the least memorable World Series since—take your pick—maybe the Blue Jays besting the Braves in six in '92 or the St. Louis Browns losing to the St. Louis Cardinals during wartime. After the Astros dismal showing in '05, the club remained what it had always been: a baseball afterthought.

Mention the Houston Astros to baseball fans around the country—before 2017, that is—and the response would likely be something about the Astrodome (derelict these many years) and possibly the team's garish but distinctive orange-and-yellow-striped rainbow jerseys (despite the fact that they were mothballed after the 1986 season).

On Chicago's North Side, let's say, ask a regular at Bernie's Tap & Grill, across from Wrigley Field, what he thinks about the team from Texas. Wait while he lowers a nearly emptied mug of Guinness, wipes his mouth with the back of a beefy paw, and concedes that, yeah, the Astros have fielded some pretty decent players over the years—Nolan Ryan, Roger Clemons, Craig Biggio, Jeff Bagwell, guys like that—and, yeah, the team has been pretty good now and then. For the most part, though, who thinks about the Houston Astros? They're a big league club in name only. Not like the Cubbies, of course.

The nation's fourth-largest city, a metropolis that sprawls across the Texas coastal plains like an ever-spreading amoeba, has supported its team for more than half a century, but even the most fanatical fan likely would concede that the Astros, before '17, were middle-aged *arrivistes*, not baseball royalty. Before George Springer, José Altuve, Carlos Correa, and the boys of hurricane summer brought home the gleaming trophy, the typical fan likely lumped the team with the Florida Marlins, the Seattle Mariners, the Arizona Diamondbacks, the Tampa Bay Rays—teams lacking the tradition and pedigree of the Yankees, Dodgers, Cards, and Giants (and, of course, the Cubs). The Astros were Macy's, not Nieman's; a Chevy, not a BMW.

With a brief tip of the cap to the city's first baseball team, the Houston Babies in 1888, forerunners to the venerable Houston Buffs of the Texas League (a St. Louis Cardinals farm team for many years and a part of Branch Rickey's minor league operation), Houston's long trek to diamond glory began on a sunny April afternoon in 1962, before the Astros were the Astros. The Houston Colt .45s, a National League expansion team, made their debut at Colt Stadium, a stadium built in five months in the middle of a parking lot, with single-level metal bleachers and lighting so dim that outfielders had to squint to home in on a fly ball sailing their way (while dodging dive-bomber mosquitoes).

The fact that the Colt .45s, be they ever so humble, existed at all was due to one of the most remarkable men in the history of the Bayou City: Roy Mark Hofheinz.

The Astros' founder, a local legend known as "the Judge," smoked 25 cigars a day—he favored Sans Souci Perfectos—drove himself around town in a black Cadillac limousine (since he couldn't find chauffeurs willing to keep his hours) and left his mark on the city in countless ways. He's best known for bringing both Major League Baseball and the Astrodome, "the Eighth Wonder of the World," to the Bayou City.

Houstonians, unless they were exasperated political rivals, found Hofheinz amusing. They had seen his like before. A couple of decades earlier, they had watched the antics of "Silver Dollar Jim" Smith, an oil man who loved tossing the coins for which he was nicknamed at people on the street while being chauffeured about town in his big, black Cadillac. Silver Dollar Jim left stacks of silver-dollar tips in restaurants and bars, tossed handfuls of gleaming silver into pools, and laughed uncontrollably as people dived in like performing seals to retrieve them. The larger-than-life Judge Hofheinz was Walter Mitty modest compared to Silver Dollar Jim.

"He was a genius and a scoundrel at the same time," Harris County Judge Ed Emmett said of Hofheinz. "He was way, way, way ahead of his time."

Hofheinz was born in Beaumont, Texas, in 1912, but the family soon moved to Houston. A yell leader in high school, he excelled at debate and always had something going, some scheme nobody else had thought of that would make him a few bucks. The propensity started early. As a nine-year-old during Prohibition, he set up a refreshment stand in his front yard, luring thirsty customers with a sign that read, "NEAR BEER SOLD HERE, BUT NO BEER SOLD NEAR HERE." As a teenage promoter, he put on alcohol-free dances for Houston's young and hip that went late into the night.

He finished high school at 15 and was planning to go to college when his father was killed driving a laundry truck. Young Roy had to go to work, which did not mean sacking groceries at the local supermarket or sweeping floors at a three-chair barbershop. He booked dance bands throughout East Texas, peddled newspapers, and sold radio air time, all while attending law school at night. He got his law degree at 19 and was elected to the Texas Legislature at 22.

At 24, Hofheinz was elected Harris County judge—the county's chief executive officer—and was the youngest man in the nation ever elected to such an office. He ran Harris County for eight energetic years but remained Judge Hofheinz the rest of his life. He paved roads, built bridges, dug tunnels under the ship channel, created a flood-control district, enacting on a local level the progressive approach to government associated with FDR. The man got things done.

In 1944, Hofheinz announced that he was taking a sabbatical from politics in order to become a millionaire. He expected it would take him about eight years. With the same energy he ruled the county, he practiced law, started wheeling and dealing in real

estate, and acquired part ownership in several radio and TV stations. He invested in a few oil wells that gave him a taste for "Texas
tea" and acquired acres and acres of open coastal prairie in and
around one of the fastest-growing cities in the nation. He made
money in the slag industry and became co-owner of the Ringling
Bros. and Barnum & Bailey Circus. Not only did he meet his millionaire mark with months to spare, he found time to serve as a
campaign manager for his old pal Lyndon Johnson, who ran for the
U.S. Senate in 1948. (That was the 86-vote victory under shadowy
South Texas circumstances that earned LBJ the sobriquet, "Land-
slide Lyndon.")

A restless millionaire several times over before age 40,
Hofheinz was elected mayor of Houston in 1952.

"With all the brashness he could muster," Al Reinert wrote in
Texas Monthly, "Hofheinz launched a public works program that
resembled a Five-Year Plan for the Roman Empire. City Hall, in the
rotund person of the mayor, was suddenly everywhere—building,
annexing, condemning, overhauling, unveiling the new Houston
International Airport. When the City Council griped bitterly about
not being consulted on any of these public endeavors, the Judge
answered blithely that, well, come to think of it, he didn't need
their help anyway."

In 1955, a frustrated City Council impeached Hofheinz, with
the support of the city attorney. When the mayor ignored them,
council members backed down and voted to censure him instead.
He went to the air waves and urged voters to toss out council
incumbents. Houstonians took his advice. They also tossed out Hiz-
zoner the Mayor.

About that time, a group of local investors was trying to land a

Major League Baseball team for Houston. Frustrated in its efforts to break into the gentlemen's club that was the MLB, the group began planning the Continental League, a third major league that would pressure baseball owners to expand the American and National Leagues. The pressure worked. In 1960, the clubby baseball establishment granted National League franchises to New York and Houston. The New York team would be the Mets, the Texas team the Colt .45s, to be owned by the Judge and his partner, R. E. "Bob" Smith.

Named after a revolver to evoke Texas's Wild West heritage, the Colt .45s were the state's first major league baseball team. (The Texas Rangers arrived in the Dallas–Fort Worth Metroplex in 1972.) Dan Rather, then a Houston TV reporter, recalled years later over dinner at Ninfa's, the venerable Mexican restaurant on Houston's east side, that the owners were looking for a name that lent itself to newspaper headline shorthand, either "Colts" or "45s."

In keeping with the frontier image, Hofheinz had his players wear blue Western-cut suits, boots, and cowboy hats when they traveled. Resembling bandleader Bob Wills and his Texas Playboys in airports and hotel lobbies around the nation did not sit well with professional baseball players. The .45s finally refused to wear the outfits. The Judge gave in.

A three-minute newsreel clip of the .45s' first game, April 10, 1962, scans the bleachers and shows men wearing snap-brimmed fedoras and short-sleeved white dress shirts, women in dresses and wide-brimmed straw hats. Seven-year-old Jeff Cohen, future executive editor of the *Houston Chronicle*, attended the game with his dad. Years later, about all he could recall were the noise and vibrations enthusiastic fans made stamping their feet on the metal bleachers. He remembered his dad having to buy membership in a "private club" beyond right field to purchase a beer, since the area was "dry" in those days. It was big league, but somehow it didn't feel like big league, particularly to those Houston baseball fans who had made summer pilgrimages over the years to St. Louis to watch the Cards, the nearest major league team to Texas until the .45s arrived.

The Cohens were among more than 25,000 fans who watched the Judge's new team easily handle Ernie Banks, Lou Brock, and the Chicago Cubs, 11–2. The Colt .45s won their first three games before expansion-team reality began to set in. They finished the season in eighth place in a 10-team league. With a record of 64–96, the out-manned gaggle of untested rookies and too-often-tested veterans finished 36½ games behind the National League champion San Francisco Giants.

The Colt .45s misfired for several years afterward, as most expansion teams do, but the Judge's front office smartly and patiently went about constructing a team of young players capable of contending for years to come—until, that is, then-general manager Spec Richardson panicked and began trading away the heart of the team. Gone were future Hall of Famer Joe Morgan, six-time All-Star Rusty Staub, Cy Young Award winner Mike Cuellar, and others. For years, the team struggled.

"We had more good young talent, I think, than any franchise in the National League, but we weren't quite mature," recalled Larry Dierker, a Colt .45s pitcher. (On his 18th birthday in 1964, in the first game he ever pitched in the majors, Dierker stuck out Willie Mays.)

When Richardson started trading away younger players to get

older players, Dierker said, "We were never able to reach maturity as a group of young players and win a championship. And it just seemed like once we made a couple of those bad ones and tried to make up for them, we continued to make deals that were not fruitful and we just never caught up until 1980." (Dierker would go on to manage the Astros and compiled the franchises' best winning percentage until A. J. Hinch's teams moved past him.)

Houstonians knew that their .45s were prelude to something bigger. (After all, the Judge was involved.) In 1960, before Houston was awarded a franchise, Hofheinz had proposed building the world's first indoor stadium as an enticement to major league sports teams intrigued by expansion into one of the nation's fastest-growing Sunbelt cities but leery of its heat, humidity, and mosquitoes. He persuaded residents of Harris County to finance the $31.6 million structure, officially known as the Harris County Domed Stadium. He would hold the 40-year lease.

Although the Dome was paid for with municipal bonds, the Judge built 53 luxury boxes with $2 million of his own money. "It was done," his son Fred Hofheinz told *Sports Illustrated*, "to attract people who used baseball games as a backdrop to sell their products." Luxury boxes designed to sequester the rich became stadium mainstays.

Hofheinz always claimed he got the idea for a covered stadium from the velarium (awning) that Roman slaves unfurled to shield wealthy visitors to the Colosseum from sun or rain. In the Judge's words, "if those Romans can put a lid on their stadium, so can we."

A more likely inspiration was Pier Luigi Nervi's multipurpose Palazzetto dello Sport in Rome, which Hofheinz had seen in *Sporting News*. A covered stadium, he claimed, would put Houston on the map: "Nobody can see [the Astrodome] and go back to Kalamazoo, Chicago, New York, you name it, and still think this town is bush league, that this town is Indian territory."

Judge Emmett, Hofheinz's successor decades later, recalled that the Judge, the ultimate salesman, won over Houston's African American community by sending sound trucks into neighborhoods with recorded messages from the likes of Hank Aaron and Willie Mays. "Want to see us play in Houston? Vote yes on the bond package," the famous voices urged. The bond measure passed narrowly, thanks in large part to black voters.

"He desegregated the city of Houston," Emmett said. "There was never any issue about race at the Astrodome."

In a town where the downtown business establishment, the religious community, and the two local newspapers worked in concert in the early 1960s to make sure that Houston would not be another Birmingham, with its high-powered water hoses and snarling police dogs, Emmett's assessment may be a bit of an overstatement, but there's no doubt that Hofheinz was progressive on racial issues. Whatever his moral stance, he knew that racial unrest was bad for business.

Hofheinz and his fellow investors considered renaming the team the Stars and their new stadium the "Stardome." Instead, the Colt .45s surrendered their guns and became the Astros in honor of nearby NASA, where scientists and engineers were four years away from sending a man to the moon. Hofheinz asked his friend Alan Shepard, the astronaut, how the Mercury crew would like having a baseball team named after them. Shepard told him they'd like it just fine.

On April 9, 1965, Hofheinz welcomed the world to the newly

christened Astrodome, the first indoor, air-conditioned stadium ever built. For the grandest of grand openings, a celebration befitting the first major league baseball game ever played indoors, he sat with his family and President Johnson and the first lady and watched the Astros play the New York Yankees in an exhibition game. Texas Governor John Connally, the Reverend Billy Graham, and 22 astronauts also were on hand. The astronauts threw out 22 ceremonial baseballs.

Graham and the other dignitaries on that April afternoon were among 47,879 fans who thrilled at the sight of the most famous Yankee of them all, future Hall of Famer Mickey Mantle, hit the first home run in the Astrodome. The Blonde Bomber's sixth-inning blast to center field landed a few yards beyond the 406-foot sign. Although Houston fans applauded the perennially injured slugger as he limped around the bases, the 474-foot-long scoreboard flashed TILT! If an Astro hit a homer, the scoreboard would produce a smoke-snorting bull, American and Texas flags flying from its horns.

The scoreboard spectacle moved irascible Cubs manager Leo Durocher to declare that "Houston is bush." Bush or not, the Astros defeated the Yankees, 2–1.

Earlier in the year, the Judge, ever the showman, had introduced the Astros' first mascot—not a cartoon character or a cavorting clown in a costume but a comedian popular at the time named Bill Dana. A regular on the *Ed Sullivan Show*, Dana would appear as the "honorary eighth astronaut, José Jiménez." Wearing a full Astros uniform for his mascot duties, he would do comedy bits before games in a faux-Spanish accent and mingle with the crowd afterward. José Jiménez didn't last long.

Neither did the grass. The Astrodome's great greenhouse ceiling, like the immense train stations of Victorian Europe, was supposed to allow enough sunlight to filter through for grass to grow, but once the Astros outfielders started losing fly balls in the glare, the transparent roof had to be painted over. The grass, of course, died, which meant that chemists had to invent "AstroTurf." A year after its opening, the Astrodome, twice as big as any single enclosure ever built, was America's third most-visited man-made attraction, after the Golden Gate Bridge and Mount Rushmore.

French ambassador Hervé Alphand was one of those visitors. He compared the steel-girdered roof of the Astrodome to the Eiffel Tower. "The Eiffel Tower is nice," agreed the Judge, "but you can't play ball there."

Graham is credited with coining the "Eighth Wonder" appellation, although he actually said: "It is in truth one of the wonders of the world." The Judge added the embellishment. The evangelist's observation came during a 10-day crusade in 1966. (During the crusade, Graham also said most Houstonians likely were going to hell.)

Not everyone loved the silvery geodesic sphere on South Main. Writer Larry McMurtry compared it to "the working end of a gigantic roll-on deodorant."

Hofheinz could tolerate the jibes. Until the end of his days, he loved the place. After his wife, Dene, died in 1966, the Judge watched his Astros in action from the office and three-story apartment he had built behind the massive scoreboard in right field. His sumptuous quarters featured massive furniture fit for a Vanderbilt, a Citizen Hearst—not to mention a billiard parlor, a miniature golf course, a beauty salon and barber shop, an interfaith chapel, a children's library, and a presidential suite reserved for LBJ, as well as bathrooms with gilded toilet seats.

Dierker, the Astros' rookie pitcher, had gotten his first glimpse of the futuristic structure—if not the Judge's lavish living quarters— a few nights before the Yankees game. "We came back from spring training, and we got back at night and when the team bus pulled up to the Astrodome, they had the lights on inside and we were all practically breathless with anticipation," he recalled. "We walked in and walked down across the concourse out into the seats and looked at the field and I remember telling somebody that I felt like I had walked into the next century because it was over and beyond anything that I ever saw."

The Astros abandoned the Dome in the final year of the old century for a newly constructed downtown ballpark (now called Minute Maid Park), and the building has stood abandoned and useless ever since. In 2005, on a playing field where Evel Knievel soared up and over 13 cars on his motorcycle, where tennis great Billie Jean King vanquished Bobby Riggs in the 1973 "Battle of the Sexes," and where Nolan Ryan threw one of his seven no-hitters, Houston briefly found a use for the Judge's Eighth Wonder of the World. Desperate Katrina survivors from New Orleans and the Gulf Coast found a haven under the Dome until they could reconstruct their lives back home or in Houston.

=====

Futuristic and fantastic the Astrodome may have been during its apogee, but NASA was more successful at making one giant leap for mankind than the Astros were at taking small steps toward baseball success. For more than a decade, the Dome was more of a draw than the team that played inside its cavernous interior.

"A ninth-place team drew two million fans that year [1965], proving that if you have a great mousetrap you can get by without a lot of cheese," writer Mickey Herskowitz observed in a column for MLB.com. "A million more paid a dollar each to see the stadium when it was empty. It seems odd now to recall how much resistance there was to the idea of an indoor ballpark. The purists feared a terrible retribution if we mortals tampered with Mother Nature. And for a while we had a wonder."

The team that played inside the Judge's wonder had come close to success 25 years earlier. Relying on the rocket right arm of the recently acquired Ryan and the knuckleball antics of veteran Joe Niekro, along with the hitting prowess of César Cedeño and José Cruz, the 1980 Astros held a three-game National League West lead over the Los Angeles Dodgers late in the season—and then promptly lost their final three games, to the Dodgers.

In a one-game playoff, Niekro came through. He allowed the Dodgers only six hits in a 7–1 Houston victory. The Astros headed to their first appearance in the National League Championship Series.

The crafty knuckleballer pitched 10 shutout innings in Game 3 of the NLCS, and the Astros defeated the Philadelphia Phillies, 1–0. Houston dared hope, but not for long. The Astros would go on to lose the series itself, three games to two. Long-suffering fans would long remember that their hometown heroes were one win away from the pennant and a trip to the 1980 World Series, but lost two straight nail-biting extra-inning games.

It would be six years before they got close again. In 1986,

strikeout artist Mike Scott pitched a September no-hitter against the Giants to clinch the NL West title. Scott's dazzling feat before a delirious home crowd set up an NLCS battle with the other 1962 expansion team, the New York Mets.

Scott, who had broken in with the Mets before being traded to the Astros, tamed former teammates Darryl Strawberry, Keith Hernandez, and Gary Carter, giving up just one run as he got credit for the win in Games 1 and 4. In Game 1, a pitching duel with Mets ace Dwight Gooden, the Astros right-hander struck out 14.

The Mets won Games 2, 3, and 5. If the Astros could somehow win Game 6, Scott, the man with the unhittable split-fingered fastball, would again take the mound for Game 7 in Houston.

It was not to be. In 16 innings, still the longest NLCS game ever, the Astros lost, 7–6. With runners at first and second, Mets left-hander Jesse Orosco struck out Kevin Bass on a curveball for the final out. The Mets would go on to defeat the Boston Red Sox, four games to three, for their first World Series triumph. The Astros waited 'til next year.

Waited for the next 18 years, actually. In 2004, an offense led by the team's fearsome "Killer Bs"—Biggio, Bagwell, Lance Berkman, and Carlos Beltrán—combined with arguably the best pitching staff in the majors—Clemons, Andy Pettitte, and Roy Oswalt—to nearly win the National League pennant. In the NLCS, the Cardinals took the first two games in St. Louis and the Astros the next three in Houston, but again it was not to be. In Game 6, the Cards' Jim Edmonds hit an extra-inning walk-off home run and made a diving over-the-shoulder catch to turn the tide of Game 7. The Cardinals won the pennant; the Astros went home to Houston. Again.

The Astros won their first National League championship a year later. After decades of frustration, they were finally in a World Series.

Unfortunately, they played like a team that had never been there before. Their opponents were the Chicago White Sox, a team that hadn't been in a World Series since the infamous "Black Sox" scandal more than a century earlier. Shoeless Joe Jackson, Eddie Cicotte, and their Black Sox teammates allegedly threw that World Series at the behest of big-time gamblers. The Astros could have used similar assistance. The White Sox swept the series.

"We couldn't pull it off ourselves, but we managed to extend a helping hand to other perennial losers," *Texas Monthly*'s John Nova Lomax observed. "The third- and fourth-longest World Series droughts in baseball history—those of the White Sox (87 years) and Phillies (77 years)—were both broken at the expense of the Astros."

Millionaire businessman Drayton McLane Jr. bought the Astros in 1992, taking ownership of a team that hadn't made the playoffs since 1986. He admitted that he had been to only a few major league games in his life but had grown up in Central Texas listening to St. Louis Cardinals games on the radio (as did many Texans, since the Cards into the late 1950s were the only major league team west of the Mississippi).

"Uncle Drayton," as he would come to be called, attended most games, sitting right behind home plate. Friendly and folksy despite his millions, he was the same guy who grew up in the wholesale grocery business in a small town. He liked to mingle with fans and players. He asked them all his favorite question: "Are you ready to be a champion?"

They were, for sure, but it just didn't happen—despite a

winning record in 13 of McLane's first 14 seasons as owner. The Astros won the NL Central Division four times in a five-year span (1997–99 and 2001). There was that NLCS in 2004 and the World Series appearance in 2005.

"All the while, generations of Astros fans were born, went to school, got married, had kids, worked away, retired, and even died off—and still the brass ring had yet to be grasped," *Texas Monthly*'s Lomax recalled. "Hell, we even had to wait in line behind the Red Sox and the Cubs."

By the time McLane decided to sell the team in 2010, he had traded away his high-priced stars (and fan favorites), attempting to lure potential buyers with a bargain-basement payroll. A former truck driver who made a fortune after loading up his U-Haul and moving to Houston in 1982 took the bait. Jim Crane bought the Astros for $680 million. The depleted 'Stros—soon to be even more depleted—were headed to baseball purgatory.

>>> A shocking scene as people slog down a flooded street after evacuating their homes because of record flooding caused by Hurricane Harvey on August 28, 2017. (Joe Raedle/Getty Images)

>>> Glenda Montelongeo, Richard Martinez, and his two young sons are helped out of a boat after being rescued near Tidwell Road and Toll Road 8 in Houston, Texas, on August 29, 2017. Rising water from Harvey forced thousands of people to rooftops or higher ground as they fled their flooded homes in Houston. (Jabin Botsford/The Washington Post via Getty Images)

>>> A boy and girl hug their grandmother's dogs as they are being rescued from dangerous rising floodwaters due to Hurricane Harvey in Spring, Texas, north of Houston, on August 28, 2017. A deluge of rain and rising floodwaters left Houston immersed and helpless. (Luke Sharrett/Bloomberg via Getty Images)

▶▶▶ Rescue workers and volunteers ferry flood victims out of a flooded Houston neighborhood in a dump truck on August 29, 2017.
(Scott Olson/Getty Images)

▶▶▶ Houston Astros center fielder Jake Marisnick #6 and left fielder Marwin Gonzalez #9 share a moment before the game against the Texas Rangers at Tropicana Field on August 29, 2017, in St. Petersburg, Florida. The game had to be played in Tropicana Field because of widespread flooding in the Houston area caused by Hurricane Harvey. The Astros were on the road when the hurricane struck Texas.
(Mike Carlson/MLB Photos via Getty Images)

▶▶▶ A young fan holds a sign of support for Houston during the game between the Texas Rangers and the Houston Astros at Tropicana Field on August 29, 2017, in St. Petersburg, Florida, because of flooding in Houston.
(Mike Carlson/MLB Photos via Getty Images)

▶▶▶ First responders stand with the Houston Astros during the national anthem on September 2, 2017, on their return to Minute Maid Park for a series against the New York Mets. The Astros were on the road when Harvey hit Texas on Aug. 25, 2017, causing record flooding in the Houston area. (Bob Levey/Getty Images)

▶▶▶ Houston Astro George Springer #4 points to a "Houston Strong" patch on his jersey after hitting a home run against the New York Mets at Minute Maid Park on September 2, 2017. "Houston Strong" quickly became a widespread slogan of solidarity in a city devastated by flooding from Hurricane Harvey, and all of the Astros wore patches on their jerseys throughout the playoffs. (Bob Levey/Getty Images)

▶▶▶ A fireplace sits in the middle of a mountainous trash pile in front of a flood-damaged home on September 5, 2017. After record rainfall hit the Houston region and other parts of Texas, residents began the long process of recovering from the storm. (Justin Sullivan/Getty Images)

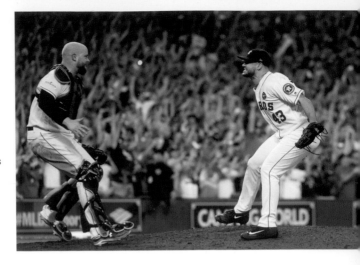

>>> And it's on to the World Series! Astros pitcher Lance McCullers Jr. #43 and catcher Brian McCann #16 celebrate after the final out of Game 7 of the American League Championship Series against the New York Yankees at Minute Maid Park on October 21, 2017. The Astros defeated the Yankees 4–0.
(Cooper Neill/MLB Photos via Getty Images)

>>> Houston Astros batting stars José Altuve #27 and Carlos Correa #1 intently watch batting practice prior to Game 1 of the 2017 World Series against the Los Angeles Dodgers at Dodger Stadium on October 24, 2017.
(Rob Tringali/MLB Photos via Getty Images)

>>> Popular Houston Texan NFL player J. J. Watt poses with Astros pitcher Dallas Keuchel #60 after throwing out the ceremonial first pitch before Game 3 of the 2017 World Series—the first game of the series at Minute Maid Park—on October 27, 2017. Watt's foundation raised more than $37 million in donations for Harvey recovery efforts. (Alex Trautwig/MLB Photos via Getty Images)

>>> Houston Astros players Carlos Correa #1, George Springer #4, and Josh Reddick #22 celebrate after the Astros defeated the Los Angeles Dodgers on October 27, 2017, in Game 3 of the World Series at Minute Maid Park. It was the first-ever World Series game win for Houston at home. (Alex Trautwig/MLB Photos via Getty Images)

>>> Astros player Derek Fisher #21 slides into home plate to score the game-winning run in the wild, 10-inning Game 5 of the 2017 World Series at Minute Maid Park on October 29, 2017. The Astros defeated the Dodgers 13–12. (Tom Pennington/Getty Images)

>>> Houston Astros player Alex Bregman #2 is mobbed by team-mates after he hit the game-winning single in Game 5 in the 10th inning. (Alex Trautwig/MLB Photos via Getty Images)

▶▶▶ Houston Astros batter Yuli Gurriel #10 tips his helmet to Dodgers pitcher Yu Darvish in the first inning of Game 7 on November 1, 2017. Gurriel caused controversy by making a racist gesture targeting Darvish in Game 3 of the Series and will be suspended for the first five games of the 2018 season.
(Kyodo News via Getty Images)

▶▶▶ Moment of victory! Houston Astros first baseman Yuli Gurriel #10 reacts after tagging out Dodger Corey Seager #5 at first base to end Game 7 with a score of 5–1 and secure a World Series championship for the Astros on November 1, 2017.
(Kevork Djansezian/Getty Images)

▶▶▶ Houston Astros players Marwin Gonzalez #9, Alex Bregman #2, José Altuve #27, and Carlos Correa #1 celebrate their World Series championship after the final out on November 1, 2017. The Astros defeated the Dodgers 5–1 to win their first World Series.
(LG Patterson/MLB Photos via Getty Images)

▶▶▶ The Houston Astros players mob each other on the field after defeating the Los Angeles Dodgers 5–1 in Game 7 to win the 2017 World Series at Dodger Stadium on November 1, 2017 in Los Angeles. (Tim Bradbury/Getty Images)

▶▶▶ Houston Astros owner Jim Crane hoists the Commissioner's Trophy during the World Series victory ceremony at Dodger Stadium on November 1, 2017. (Kevork Djansezian/Getty Images)

⟩⟩⟩ Houston Astros ace pitcher Justin Verlander and fiancée model Kate Upton snap a victory selfie on the field at Dodger Stadium as they celebrate the Astros' World Series championship. (Ezra Shaw/Getty Images)

⟩⟩⟩ Back in Houston, Astros fans are ecstatic as they watch their team win the World Series on a giant high-definition TV at Minute Maid Park. (Bob Levey/Getty Images)

⟩⟩⟩ Two days later, November 3, 2017, the Astros celebrate with their fans at a parade in downtown Houston. (Ken Murray/Icon Sportswire via Getty Images)

CHAPTER 11

Crane Finds His Billy Beane

Heresy was good: heresy meant opportunity.

MICHAEL LEWIS, *MONEYBALL: THE ART OF*

WINNING AN UNFAIR GAME

Had you checked the nightstands beside the king-size beds of baseball executives in the early years of the 21st century, chances are you'd find a copy of Michael Lewis's *Moneyball*, published in 2003. Immensely readable and entertaining, even for readers who wouldn't know an ERA from an OPS (the sum of on-base and slugging percentages), Lewis's book tells the story of the transformation of the Oakland A's, a small-market team that figured out how to use advanced statistics in player evaluation— data that offers previously unknown insights into how players contribute to winning—to gain a competitive advantage. Despite being underfinanced, the team from the other side of the San Francisco Bay found success at a fraction of the price that it cost traditional big spenders like the New York Yankees and the Los Angeles Dodgers (thus "moneyball").

Lewis's hero is Oakland general manager Billy Beane, once an athlete with fantastic potential whose Major League Baseball career with the New York Mets—lifetime batting average .219, home runs 3—had been a bust. Beane, Lewis writes, "is a man whose life was turned upside down by professional baseball, and who, miraculously, found a way to return the favor."

Beane's antagonists, as Lewis tells the tale, were crusty, old baseball scouts, leathery-faced guys—usually former players—who believed "you found a big league ballplayer by driving sixty thousand miles, staying in a hundred crappy motels, and eating god knows how many meals at Denny's all so you could watch 200 high school and college baseball games inside of four months, 199 of which were completely meaningless to you."

That's the way it was and always had been. Players, high school and college, could always spot the scouts in the crowd—the poker-faced intensity, the pencil and notebook, the comfortable khaki pants and jacket. With the faith and determination of grizzled prospectors, they expected to find, someday, the next Henry Louis Gehrig playing high-school ball for the New York School of Commerce, the next Mickey Charles Mantle on the playing fields of Commerce, Oklahoma.

"The old scouts are like a Greek chorus; it is their job to underscore the eternal themes of baseball," Lewis writes. "The eternal themes are precisely what Billy Beane wants to exploit for profit—by ignoring them."

Beane ignored them by taking his eye off the ball—and bat—and focusing on the numbers, computer-generated numbers that he insisted told him a whole lot more about a ball player than what a scout could discern in person. Those numbers had become available only a few years earlier through the pioneering work of baseball statistics savant Bill James and others of like mind. In fact, so much information became available so quickly, once the statisticians got interested, that it threatened to overwhelm teams that might be interested.

Beane was more than interested. Because the A's could not afford superstars, they needed a different approach, a more analytical approach. Relying on close statistical analysis, the team developed a new set of hiring criteria, and instead of relying on the idiosyncratic observations of old-time scouts, Beane's A's turned to computer nerds from Harvard and other such places, most of whom had never played the game.

Peering into their laptops, the statisticians found more precise and accurate metrics. They discovered, for example, that the way the game traditionally had scored errors was basically meaningless as a metric for a team's long-term success. (A player might make fewer errors because he's too slow to make a play on a ball hit in his vicinity.)

They found that batting average, a metric used at least since Wee Willie Keeler "hit 'em where they ain't" in the early 1900s, was actually an unreliable predictor of future performance. Dig out on-base percentage and slugging percentage and you have more accurate predictors; those metrics reflect a hitter's pitch selection and power, which are repeatable skills. That finding alone has revolutionized baseball strategy.

By the time Jim Crane bought the failing Houston Astros in 2011, some version of Beane's analytic approach was de rigueur among the teams having the most success. The Astros were not among them. When Crane bought the team, it was still relying on manual reports from its scouts.

Crane also investigated several of the more successful clubs before signing his name on the dotted line. The analytics approach they had adopted appealed to his businessman's bottom-line mentality. It seemed trim, clean, and scientific.

Lewis's book—and certainly the hit movie of the same name starring Brad Pitt and Jonah Hill—exaggerated the tension between Luddite scouts going with their gut and sophisticated young statisticians dissecting the game from unlikely angles, but there was no doubt that analytics was here to stay. The challenge was to bridge the gap between old-school baseball men and the number crunchers, few of whom had ever set a spiked foot in a batter's box or thrown a ball on a line to first base.

However difficult the transition—some teams were successful, some weren't—data-driven decision making and performance measurement were revolutionizing the search for talent, player development, trade strategy, and, when managers bought into the new approach, in-game decisions. Not only Beane's A's, but also the St. Louis Cardinals, the Boston Red Sox, the Tampa Bay Rays, the Philadelphia Phillies, the Atlanta Braves, and the Chicago Cubs had implemented some version of data-driven baseball by 2011.

Tom Verducci, in his 2017 book about the Cubs' ascent—*The Cubs Way: The Zen of Building the Best Team in Baseball and Breaking the Curse*—describes a 2012 meeting of Cubs personnel in the ballroom of a budget hotel in Mesa, Arizona. The team's new president of baseball operations, Theo Epstein, gave a long speech in which he outlined how the Cubs were going to win the World Series. Since the young front-office prodigy had built two World Series championship teams in Boston as an early practitioner of analytics principles, his audience—managers, coaches, instructors, scouts, trainers, analysts, and so forth—tended to listen. As Verducci points out, they were probably worried about whether their jobs were safe under a new regime—with good reason—but they also knew that the young man at the front of the hotel ballroom had proved himself in accursed Boston (86 years between championships). Maybe he could do the same in the Windy City, bereft since 1908.

Epstein told them he wanted an offense that "boasted a relentless batting order, not one reliant simply on its few big hitters in the middle." He also wanted a sterling defense.

He said he wanted a "pitching staff populated by pitchers who threw a heavy percentage of strikes but also featured swing-and-miss stuff." He wanted "a baseball operations department that would be the best in baseball."

Finally, he said, he wanted players with character: "We're not going to compromise character for talent.... We're the Cubs. We're going to have both. Talent and character."

The Cubs got what they wanted: a World Series victory in 2016. A year after the denizens of Wrigley Field entrusted their fate to Epstein, it was Crane's turn. A businessman who appreciated numbers, he was aware of moneyball and was willing to go all in with the analytics approach to building a team. First, he had to find his own Billy Beane. He met him in St. Louis.

Jeff Luhnow, the man Crane hired as his general manager, was the very model of the *Moneyball* paradigm. And he had read the book.

"My ex-wife bought it for me," he told writer Howard Megdal, who interviewed him for his 2016 book, *The Cardinals Way: How One Team Embraced Tradition and Moneyball at the Same Time.* "My birthday's June 8th. The book had just come out. I was in the Bay Area, so there was a lot of talk about it on the radio. I got the book. Read it front to back. I was interested, but that was about it."

Luhnow—pronounced LOO-no—also had a lifelong interest in baseball. He was born in 1966 in Mexico City, where his parents ran a publishing business and were baseball fans, especially his mother. A dual citizen, he attended an American school and rooted for the Dodgers as a kid. He even visited the Astrodome when he came to Texas for summer camp.

Despite his childhood interest in the game, his academic pedigree didn't obviously point back to baseball. Luhnow graduated from Penn with degrees in economics and engineering and received an MBA from the Kellogg School of Management at Northwestern University. For a class in management strategy, however, he studied the Chicago Cubs and supplemented his research "by spending many afternoons in the bleachers drinking Old Style Beer and yelling at Sammy Sosa. So I learned a lot about the business side of baseball, as well as the fan experience," he told Megdal. He also was a fanatical fantasy baseball player.

After college, he worked as a consultant at McKinsey & Company in Chicago and a few years later as general manager and vice president of marketing at PetStore.com. He also led a California company called Archetype Solutions that developed algorithms for custom-made clothing for brands like Lands' End. He was a business-turnaround expert, and with his graying, closely cropped hair and his focus on measurables, discipline, and regimentation, he fit the organization-guy stereotype.

On a 2003 trip to Cincinnati to pitch to investors, Luhnow reconnected with an old Chicago friend named Jay Kern. As Tyler Kepner of the *New York Times* tells the story, Kern's father-in-law, Jim DeWitt Jr., happened to be the owner of the St. Louis Cardinals and, like most baseball men, was mesmerized by Michael Lewis's newly published best seller. The Cards had built a successful franchise largely through astute trades for veterans, but DeWitt had concluded that the analytics approach *Moneyball* laid out was a more sustainable business model. He named Luhnow vice president in 2003.

Luhnow was 37 when he walked away from Southern California startups and venture capitalists with fetch money for pet food companies. He'd never played baseball above the high-school level, never worked a single day in baseball at any level. And he was going to one of the most successful franchises in baseball. To change it.

"I never really intended to get into baseball," Luhnow said. "I worked as an engineer. I've always been at baseball games. I've been around it.... After a few conversations, I met a few people and decided to quit my job and become a baseball executive."

Easy decision, right? Maybe so, but the rookie executive had a tough time his first few years with the Cardinals.

"He certainly wasn't universally accepted," DeWitt told writer Megdal. "Anytime you make a change in an organization that's different from the direction that it's been headed—and especially one that's had a lot of success—I mean, you're going to get pushback. I did get pushback, but I wasn't going to change, because I knew in the end that it was something that had to be done."

Luhnow didn't know the baseball culture, and, more worrisome for the young executive, his presence threatened people, particularly old-time scouts and the Cardinals' longtime general manager Walt Jocketty. Nevertheless, Luhnow knew the owner had his back, plus he put in the time and effort to learn, both the game and the culture. Named director of amateur scouting in 2005, he visited minor league affiliates, sat in on instructional meetings and interviewed every scout. He also put together a singularly successful draft operation.

That same year, Luhnow hired a former Lake Tahoe blackjack dealer and NASA engineer named Sig Mejdal, a mathematician with two master's degrees from San Jose State University—in operations research and cognitive psychology—and a passion for baseball. At NASA, Mejdal was a biomathematician in the Fatigue Countermeasures Group. He studied the effects of sleep loss and jet lag and investigated optimal sleep patterns for astronauts on the International Space Station.

Mejdal had read *Moneyball* as well, and he hoped that baseball was beginning to recognize that someone like him, someone with a passion for numbers, baseball, and baseball numbers, might prove useful. After sending out resumes and proposals and traveling to the 2003 winter baseball meetings in New Orleans, an executive finally bit. Luhnow hired him to run the Cardinals' new analytics department.

Ironically, Luhnow and Mejdal were joining a team that had originated baseball analytics—a hundred years earlier. The legendary Branch Rickey—Cardinals general manager for 23 years, inventor of the baseball farm system, and the man who, as the Brooklyn Dodgers general manager, signed Jackie Robinson—hired a statistician in 1914 to chart every game, "with base and out efficiency in mind." Needless to say, Rickey didn't have a computer or videotaping capabilities that could discern the spin direction on Dizzy Dean's '30s-era curveballs.

From 2004 through 2011, the Cardinals would draft more players who made it to the major leagues than any other organization. Of the 25 players on the team's 2011 World Series roster, 16 were drafted during the Luhnow regime, although by the time the Cards defeated the Texas Rangers in a thrilling seven-game World Series, Luhnow himself was long gone to the Lone Star State.

By then the Cardinals franchise had become, in Kepner's words, "the model organization: a mid-market behemoth with a steady pipeline of high-impact prospects who allowed the team to afford luxury items at the top of a modest payroll. The Cardinals ranked with Beane's A's, the Tampa Bay Rays—led by Wall Street veterans—and others among the more technologically savvy organizations."

Crane hired Luhnow on a tip from Peter Ueberroth, the former baseball commissioner who was a golfing partner at Pebble Beach. Ueberroth knew Luhnow through a family connection.

Crane had interviewed at least eight candidates, most of them assistant general managers. Ueberroth told Crane he never would have found Luhnow by looking at the top of the org chart. The

Astros' new owner was intrigued, even though Luhnow didn't have the resume that older, more experience execs had compiled. The candidate from the Cardinals also brought with him a 20-plus page treatise on how to fix the Astros. For Crane, that detailed analysis was key. He knew that Luhnow was his man.

Along with his "how to build a winner in Houston" book, Luhnow brought Mejdal with him to be director of the Decision Sciences Department. (I think it's safe to say that John J. McGraw, Leo Durocher, and Casey Stengel did not have a Decision Sciences Department.) As he had done in St. Louis, Mejdal's objective was to make analytics the primary decision-driver at every level of team operations, from scouting and player development to building the team's international program (primarily Latin America).

He brought with him metrics that were still relatively foreign to the Astros operation. Now, the Astros, and every other team, use such esoteric criteria as a batter's walk rate, his on-base percentage (OBP), and his weighted on-base average or woba (pronounced Whoa-buh) to arrive at a single score for making a precise data-driven decision on personnel. As recently as 2011, when Luhnow and Mejdal showed up in Houston, the team hadn't quite figured out how to acquire or use such information.

Like hitting on 16 against a blackjack dealer's 7, Ben Reiter of *Sports Illustrated* noted, the Astros vowed to make the smart decision, even if it didn't feel right, whether that meant letting go of a fan-favorite player or drafting a player baseball traditionalists considered risky. If the numbers said do it, the Astros would trust the numbers. Other teams were taking the analytics approach as well, but the Astros were more committed than most.

A reporter for *Houstonia* magazine wrote that the actual process looked a whole lot like telemarketing: "five youngish-looking guys sitting inside a stale conference room, hunched over computer screens, surrounded by whiteboards scrawled with names, numbers and brain-bending equations. Officially known as 'The Decisions Sciences Department,' and more popularly as 'The Room That Moneyball Built,' it's a place of soft bodies and pocket protectors, of advanced degrees in statistics and computer science, and it sits on the fifth floor of Minute Maid Park, about 450 feet from home plate and yet somehow millions of miles away."

The Astros' new general manager also hired a 31-year-old Yale graduate named Mike Elias to be the team's new director of amateur scouting; Elias had worked in the Cardinals' scouting department. As his assistant GM, Luhnow hired David Stearns, a 29-year-old Harvard graduate who had most recently worked for the Indians. The new director of pro scouting was Kevin Goldstein, who had never worked in professional baseball.

He also would eventually hire as his field manager a Stanford University psychology major with baseball savvy and experience and a respect for analytics. A. J. Hinch was a perfect fit for Luhnow and for the team as a whole.

Luhnow pledged to Crane to basically deconstruct an organization that had lost 106 games in 2011 and would lose even more in each of the next two seasons. Deconstruct and then reconstruct.

He told Crane he would rebuild the Astros' depleted minor league system. He would restock the major league roster with players acculturated on Astros farm teams, young players who would be under team salary control for a maximum length of time. Then, when they needed to, they would add veteran players to the mix. Analytics would determine who those players were and when to move them up. Crane gave him time.

"That just doesn't happen very often in sports," Bill Brown, the Astros' longtime TV announcer wrote in 2017, recalling how, five years earlier, Crane had called him into his office and laid out the plan Luhnow had concocted and he had agreed to.

It doesn't happen very often, because it's a multi-season project, and all kinds of things can interfere. "Players go down with injuries," Brown noted. "People in the front office leave for more attractive jobs with competitors, creating a brain drain. Owners shortcut their long-range plans, getting impatient and going for quick results. Jim Crane stuck with the plan."

Or it doesn't happen because owners and general managers fall in love with the players who have gone to battle for them over the years. That's what happened with Crane's predecessor, Drayton McLane Jr., one of his front-office people told me. His stars—Craig Biggio, Jeff Bagwell, and others—may have lost a step or two, but McLane was reluctant to let them go, analytics be damned. That wouldn't happen with Crane or Luhnow, who rely on at least 50 weighted criteria—including off-the-field behavior—to measure a player's worth. If the numbers say keep him, they do; if the numbers say otherwise, they don't, with rare exceptions.

The new era of analytics wasn't just restricted to decision-making about the roster. The Astros, like other teams, also began pushing data onto the field of play, and Hinch, with two computers in the dugout, has access to all the information he needs.

His team evolved into MLB's most enthusiastic practitioner of "the shift," using the club's proprietary database to position their defenders on the field in combinations that looked absurd and almost sacrilegious to baseball purists. Years ago, their purist predecessors had grumbled when teams played the pull-hitting Ted Williams of the Boston Red Sox by shifting to the right—they argued it wasn't fair—but now the Astros shifted on almost every hitter. Watch José Altuve quickly consult the notes he keeps in his cap as a hitter walks to the plate. He's relying on spray charts the Astros' database has compiled for every hitter on every pitch count against every type of pitch thrown by every type of pitcher.

It's a wonder Altuve doesn't need a 10-gallon hat, although Hinch and his coaches have a feel for those players who know how to incorporate the information into their game and those who tend to get bogged down. They try to dispense what they need to know in digestible components.

Altuve will know, let's say, that on a certain left-handed pull hitter, the numbers might dictate that he move into shallow right field, with shortstop Carlos Correa sliding to his left until he's waiting for the pitch behind second base itself. Trusting in the percentages, the Astros' sabermetricians are confident they have defenders covering the exact spots on the field where batted balls most likely will be hit. Of course, the batter might decide to fight the shift by trying to hit to the opposite field, but if that's his choice, the Astros defense already has won. They have forced the hitter out of his "heat map," robbed him of his power.

Megdal contended that the Astros may have been early and enthusiastic practitioners, but other teams quickly caught up once they realized its effectiveness. "Innovation, by definition, suggests change will be taking place," he told Reiter of *Sports Illustrated*.

If there's change taking place, it's not likely going to feel right at first. If it felt right, it would have been done a long time ago."

The shift to the shift throughout baseball has transformed the way the game is played. Because the maneuver cuts off the possibility of batted balls scooting through a hole in the infield or dropping in for a Texas Leaguer, hitters started trying to "launch' the ball into the air. They struck out more. And yet the odds dictated the success of balls soaring skyward—and maybe out of the park.

Teams can play their infielders wherever they want to—some anticipate teams using a fourth outfielder in the not-too-distant future—but the one ball they'll never catch is the one that lands in the seats. The introduction in 2015 of Statcast, MLB's camera-based analytics system, has confirmed the significance of the "launch angle," a measurement of a ball's vertical trajectory.

Attention to the launch angle has revived careers, including Chris Taylor, the Dodgers' infielder/outfielder and his teammate Justin Turner, the barbarian-bearded third baseman. It has turned spray hitters into sluggers, including a little second baseman for the Astros who happened to be the American League MVP.

———————

"The games are games of odds," an expert on baseball analytics wrote in 2009. "Like professional card counters, the modern thinkers want to play the odds as efficiently as they can; but of course to play the odds efficiently they must first know the odds. Hence the new statistics, and the quest to acquire new data, and the intense interest in measuring the impact of every little thing a player does on his team's chances of winning."

That expert was none other than Michael Lewis, in a *New York Times Magazine* article. Lewis was writing, not about baseball or the A's or the Astros, but about another Houston sports franchise, one that had transformed itself into an analytics pioneer before Crane and the Astros bought into the new numbers game. In 2005, the NBA's Houston Rockets owner Leslie Alexander, a Wall Street investor, went looking for new management willing to take over his losing team and rethink the game. As his general manager, he hired Daryl Morey, a young entrepreneur with a degree from MIT's Sloan School of Management. Morey had read the groundbreaking work of baseball metrics genius Bill James, and he yearned to own a professional sports franchise where he could apply James' analytics approach.

"We now have all this data," Alexander told Lewis. "And we have computers that can analyze that data. And I wanted to use that data in a progressive way. When I hired Daryl, it was because I wanted somebody that was doing more than just looking at players in the normal way. I mean, I'm not even sure we're playing the game the right way."

In 2001, Morey was working for a Boston consulting firm called Parthenon, when a group trying to buy the Red Sox turned to him for advice. The Red Sox bid failed, but a related group bought the Boston Celtics and hired Morey to help reorganize the storied franchise.

"In addition to figuring out where to set ticket prices, Morey helped to find a new general manager and new people looking for better ways to value basketball players," Lewis wrote in the *New York Times* article. "The Celtics improved. Leslie Alexander heard whispers that Morey, who was 33, was out in front of those trying to rethink the game, so he hired him to remake the Houston Rockets."

What Morey did for the Rockets was not unlike what Beane had done for the A's a decade before. Relying on analytics, he found ways to improve the team without spending huge amounts of money.

At Minute Maid Park, a few blocks from the Rockets' home, the first key components of the Luhnow plan already were in the talent pipeline when Crane bought the team. Pitcher Dallas Keuchel, drafted in 2009, was a Cy Young winner his second season with the Astros. Altuve and George Springer, both drafted in 2011, got better every year. The next wave included Correa, Lance McCullers Jr., both drafted in 2012, Derek Fisher in 2014, and Alex Bregman, drafted in 2015. All would play key roles in the Astros' championship season.

"Not everybody bought into what we were doing," Luhnow would tell the *Houston Chronicle* after the early years in the baseball wilderness. "[Crane] and I met with season-ticket holders to explain that we were going to be transparent, that we were going to be honest, that this would take time and that there would be rough patches, and there were."

The most nettlesome patch was, arguably, the 2013 draft, when Luhnow and his analytics gurus selected pitcher Mark Appel as the first overall selection, instead of University of San Diego third baseman Kris Bryant. Appel, a big-bodied thrower from Stanford University, had grown up in West Houston and—perhaps just as important as his potential—didn't have much contract leverage as a college senior.

"This is the most significant investment the Astros have made

in their history to an amateur player, and we hope we're invest-
ing a lot in him in the future," Luhnow said when he announced
the Appel signing. "We believe it's going to be a long-term
relationship."

It wasn't. The young man from the neighborhood never threw a
pitch for the Astros. After Appel struggled for three seasons in the
Astros' minor league system, the team traded him to Philadelphia
in a deal to acquire relief pitcher Ken Giles, Meanwhile, Bryant,
whom the Cubs chose as the second overall selection, would go on
to be named the National League Rookie of the Year in 2015. A year
later, in the wake of the Cubs' World Series victory, Bryant was
named the National League's Most Valuable Player.

Luhnow and the analytics also missed on J. D. Martinez, the
slugger who in 2017 hit 45 homers—including four in one game—
for the Tigers and Diamondbacks, while registering a .690 slugging
percentage. The Astros had him in 2014 but released him after
spring training. He just couldn't hit as an Astro. After he left Houston, he figured out what he was doing wrong.

The traditionalists, those who resented systems-man Luhnow,
might credit his predecessor, Ed Wade, now a Phillies executive.
Wade, they noted, was the guy who drafted Keuchel and Springer
and signed Altuve.

No way, says Charlie Pallilo, a longtime sports radio broadcaster with a keen baseball mind. "A blind squirrel," he told Roy
Bragg of the *San Antonio Express-News*, "can find an acorn every
once in a while." Bragg agreed, labeling Luhnow "a baseball
brainiac."

Nevertheless, Luhnow skeptics lurked inside the organization, and their suspicion had not been dispelled when Reiter, the

writer, showed up in 2014 to laud the Astros' approach to analytics. Luhnow and his computer-savvy cohorts were still viewed as "know-it-all baseball outsiders," even though they had been in baseball for more than a decade and had achieved success in St. Louis. The naysayers pointed to Appel and other draftees on which Luhnow and his vaunted system had whiffed.

"Worst of all," Reiter wrote in *Sports Illustrated*, "Luhnow and his execs were openly violating the baseball compact by which rebuilding teams were supposed to obscure their long-term plan by maintaining the illusion that they were genuinely trying to win each and every year, even if it meant losing just a little less."

In Luhnow's first two seasons as general manager, the Astros won 106 games and lost 218. An Astros fan blog noted in 2012: "Crane appears to have no interest in putting together a team that is competitive, at least at this point." The team was accused of flouting, in Reiter's words, "the most basic element of a baseball team's social compact—that it tries its best to win every game."

Then-Astros bench coach and former Baltimore manager Dave Trembley (who, along with manager Bo Porter, would be deposed in 2014) described an Astros version of the tension Lewis dramatized in *Moneyball.* "I think what you see," the *Houston Chronicle* reported Trembley saying in a radio interview, "is you see a distinct difference" between coaches, managers, and instructors "who have been in the game for an awful long time" and those "in the front office."

Trembley continued: "They rely heavily on analytics. I know in Houston they rely heavily on what they call the model, and the computer. They have a lot of good ideas, but there is a definite separation, I would say, of church and state. They feel as if their way is the right way, and baseball people—I think what baseball people want is they want their opinion to be asked and their experience to be respected and appreciated and I think that's really what was the disconnect in Houston."

Luhnow forged ahead despite the challenges on field and off. He echoed Brown in his praise of Crane. "He stuck with the plan. He trusted the people in baseball operations. He said that when the time came, he would support us with resources. He did that."

During those two seasons, a combined 3.3 million fans trooped into Minute Maid to watch the most woeful team in the majors, a total not much beyond the 3 million-plus who watched the Astros play in 2007 alone. Local TV ratings for some of the games in 2013 were 0.0, although broadcaster Brown disputed those dismal ratings. "I know my mother-in-law was watching," he wrote.

Like a late-winter flu, the misery lingered. In 2011, the Astros lost 106 games. They lost 107 in 2012, and 111 in 2013, their first season in the American League.

"We spent more time talking about the top minor leaguers and their exploits at Quad Cities and Corpus Christi than we spent on the major league club many nights," Brown recalled. "Crowds were sparse, and interest in the team was almost nonexistent."

Signing a few veterans in an effort to win a few more games might have provided a temporary salve for the perennial pain, but Crane hung in. However tempting it might have been to haul out his checkbook and avoid the embarrassment of yet another losing team, he understood that building a successful franchise was a long-term project, particularly in an era of free agency.

Crane never had doubts about staying the course. It didn't seem all that long to him.

However impatient he and Luhnow might have been, they could console themselves in 2014, despite the losses, when the Astros became the first team to have the first pick in three consecutive amateur drafts. This was never a goal, they told Reiter, but a by-product of their long-term plan—a plan that came to glorious fruition, as Reiter predicted, in 2017.

CHAPTER 12

Greatest Game Ever

ASTROS LEAD SERIES, 3-2

This game!!!!!!

JUSTIN TIMBERLAKE ON TWITTER

For a team that loves numbers, the numbers for Game 5 of the 2017 World Series were pretty head-scratching. Five hours and 17 minutes, the second-longest game in World Series history. A game that began Sunday night and ended Monday morning. Fourteen pitchers throwing 417 pitches. Twenty-eight hits. Twenty-five runs. Seven home runs. The Astros' final game at Minute Maid in 2017 became the climactic moment in the team's 56-year history (for a few days, that is).

Longtime baseball watchers seemed to be in a daze, and it wasn't just the late hour when Game 5 ended that had them reeling. "I have covered every World Series game since 1975. Game 5 was the most insanely entertaining I have ever seen," *Washington Post* columnist Tom Boswell proclaimed the morning after. "That's not the same thing as 'best,' a distinction usually reserved for World Series games with the highest stakes, such as the torturously thrilling Game 7 just 361 days ago when the Cubs won their first title in 108 years. The amazements of Game 5 fall into a different category: glorious games of continuous disbelief when all our baseball expectations, built over our lifetimes, are shredded by an unseen clown and tossed in our grinning faces."

"Miraculous drama and unabashed kookiness," is how Boswell's counterpart out west, Bill Plaschke of the *Los Angeles Times*, described the Series. "This World Series is driving you bonkers, and there's nothing you can do about it," he wrote.

Carlos Correa, the Astros' 23-year-old superstar, couldn't believe what he had just lived through. "I feel like I'm going to have a heart attack out there. It's [so] high-pressure," he said. "The game is going back and forth. Both teams are great, scoring runs. Hopefully we can win one more game and take a break, because this is hard on me."

"Just when I thought I could describe Game 2 as my favorite game of all time, I think Game 5 exceeded that and more," Astros manager A. J. Hinch said. "It's hard to put into words all the twists and turns in that game—the emotion, doing it at home, in front of our home crowd."

Fans loved the game for all its craziness—particularly Astros fans—but it gave baseball purists pause. All the home runs and the power pitchers suggested to them that baseball itself was changing, and not for the better. More and more 100-mile-per-hour pitchers and more and more hitters who either swung for the fences or struck out—the launch-angle era, it has come to be called—meant that some of the subtleties of the game would be forgotten.

And maybe so, but with two thoroughbreds, both Cy Young

Award winners, on the mound for Game 5, nobody was predicting a slugfest. Here was finesse pitcher Dallas Keuchel, at home, where his ERA in 57 starts since 2014 was 2.32. In three previous playoff starts at Minute Maid, he had allowed two runs in 19⅔ innings for an astounding 0.92 ERA. And here was Clayton Kershaw, three-time Cy Young winner, seven-time All-Star and arguably the best pitcher in baseball.

Predictions evaporated early. Keuchel gave up a leadoff single to Chris Taylor and then with one out, he issued back-to-back walks to Justin Turner and Kike Hernández. He struck out Cody Bellinger, but Logan Forsythe stroked a two-out single to left that brought in two runs.

Forsythe left too soon on a stolen-base attempt, and Keuchel threw to first to try to pick him off. The runner was stranded between bases, and Yuli Gurriel threw wildly to José Altuve at second. As Altuve struggled to snare the ball and then get back to the bag to tag Forsythe, Hernández raced in from third to score, increasing LA's lead to 3–0. The Astros' analytics gurus probably knew that Kershaw's career record in games in which he is spotted a three-run lead was 124–19.

Houston failed to score in the first inning and remained scoreless until the fourth. In the top of the fourth, Keuchel was working with two outs and a runner on second, having settled into a quiet pitchers' duel with Kershaw after a rough top of the first inning. But Austin Barnes, perhaps the Dodgers' weakest hitter, singled on a liner to left, which brought Forsythe home from second, extending the Los Angeles lead to 4–0. Charlie Culberson legged out an infield single, and Hinch decided enough was enough, pulling his starter from the game after he recorded just 11 outs. Luke

Gregerson came on in relief and struck out Taylor on a checked swing to end the inning.

The Astros got to Kershaw in the bottom of the fourth. George Springer walked. Altuve slapped a single and Correa hit a double that sent Springer home. With Altuve on first and Correa on third, the score 4–1, Gurriel, who had struggled against left-handers, came to the plate. Bat held high, he powered Kershaw's first pitch, a fastball, over the left field wall. Alex Bregman told a radio audience weeks later about a subtle, little glance he happened to notice from Gurriel out toward Kershaw, as if he were saying, "I can do this all day."

Game tied at 4. The fun was just beginning.

Astros reliever Collin McHugh walked Corey Seager and Turner. After striking out Hernández, he served up a fast ball to Bellinger, and the 22-year-old rookie knocked the ball over the right field wall for a three-run homer. Dodgers 7, Astros 4.

"Biggest no-nos in pitching: Don't walk the leadoff batter in an inning and don't give back a lead after your batters have worked to tie a game or go ahead," *New York Times* blogger Dave Waldstein noted. "McHugh did it all, and the Houston fans are quiet and depressed again."

In the bottom of the fifth, Kershaw got two quick outs and then walked Springer and Bregman in succession. That was all for the Dodgers' ace, as manager Dave Roberts called on reliever Kenta Maeda to face Altuve. With a 3–2 count, Altuve smashed the game's third three-run homer. Out in right field, train conductor Bobby Dynamite blew the whistle and sent the locomotive down the track yet again. Score tied, 7–7.

"It's hard to adequately describe the complete energy shifts that have taken place in this building," Waldstein noted, "first with Gurriel's 3-run homer, then Bellinger's 3-run homer dampening it down, and then Altuve's reigniting the thunderous cheers.

"The fans were chanting M.V.P. with a deep, throaty insistence, and Altuve put everything he had into one mighty swing from his diminutive body. The ball went about 450 feet down the left field line, but foul. Then, on the next pitch from Maeda, Altuve straightened it out. Swinging as hard as he could again, he blasted the ball about as high as it was long and the fans, led by base runner Springer with his arms aloft, erupted.

"Quite a buzz in here now. Everyone knows they are witnessing a remarkable game in a fun World Series."

Neither team scored in the sixth inning. In the seventh, Bellinger stroked a hit to center field that got past Springer. Trying to make a diving catch, he allowed Bellinger to reach third and Hernández to score. Dodgers 8, Astros 7, briefly.

Leading off the bottom of the seventh, Springer made up for his misplay of Bellinger's RBI triple. He smashed a home run on the first pitch.

"That was a very angry swing," Springer said afterward. "I was upset at the bad decision I made [defensively]. That's a very lonely feeling to know that I made a bad decision. I'll own up to it. I should've stopped. But I got told by Alex Cora and A. J. Hinch, 'It's over. Just go have a good quality at bat and see what happens.' To go from that low to that high is very emotional. I don't really know how to describe it."

The seventh inning wasn't over. Bregman slapped a single and Altuve a double, scoring Bregman with no outs. Astros 9, Dodgers 8.

With Correa at bat, a wild pitch allowed Altuve to scamper to third base. On the next pitch, the Astros shortstop hit a home run into the Crawford Boxes in left field, widening the Astros' lead to 11–8.

Lifelong Astros fan David Fahrenthold, the *Washington Post* reporter attending a couple of games with his dad, happened to be sitting near the box occupied by denizens of the "Nerd Cave," the mathematicians and sabermetricians behind the team's vaunted analytics strategy. He noticed that, unlike most fans, they wore suits and ties. Instead of watching the actual game, they stared into their phones and merely listened. He was close enough to tell they were incessantly checking Twitter for esoteric bits of information about history, precise circumstance, tendencies. Only toward the end of the marathon contest, as the craziness reached its peak, did he notice the nerds loosen their ties and lift their eyes toward the action on the field.

The rest of the park was rocking as the Astros extended their lead. In the midst of the celebrating, it took a while for fans, players, and umpires to notice the shirtless man with "Villains Never Die" scrawled across his chest cavorting on the field. Wearing a "Villain" baseball cap and Stars and Stripes biker shorts, he was quickly swarmed by security behind second base. He turned out to be Vitaly Zdorovetskiy, a YouTube favorite for his prank videos. In 2016, he was arrested for climbing the Hollywood sign and for running onto the court during Game 4 of the NBA Finals. Zdorovetskiy was cuffed and led out of the park, allowing the sanctioned craziness on the field to continue. Dodgers reliever Tony Cingrani brought the seventh to a close with no more scoring.

In the top of the eighth, two doubles, one from Joc Pederson and the other from Seager, made the score 11–9. In the bottom of the inning, Brian McCann hit another home run, making the score 12–9. Astros fans dared to dream: surely they could hold on to a three-run lead.

It was the top of the ninth, the score reaching sandlot proportions and it still wasn't over. Hinch looked past struggling reliever Ken Giles, and instead sent Chris Devenski back to the mound after he recorded one out in the eighth. Devenski walked Bellinger, struck out Forsythe, and then allowed a one-handed home run to Puig.

Astros 12, Dodgers 11, and the inning continued. Barnes hit a double. Pederson grounded out to short, and Taylor walked to the plate. On a 2–2 count, he singled to center, scoring Barnes. Seager flied out to center to end the torture Astros fans were enduring. The Dodgers had clawed their way back from their third deficit of three or more runs. Astros 12, Dodgers 12.

The Twitter world was delirious. "This game is craaaaa-zzzzzyy!!!!! #WorldSeries2017," Chris Paul, the newest Houston Rocket, tweeted. "This game is insane," J. J. Watt echoed. Justin Timberlake could hardly find the words. "This game!!!!!!"

The Astros came up empty in the bottom half of the inning, and Minute Maid seemed to take a collective breath. The noise subsided, briefly.

Columnist Boswell tried to imagine what the players themselves were thinking at this point: "Many teams in many sports respect each other. But the Houston Astros and Los Angeles Dodgers almost seem in awe of their foes and, a bit sheepishly, of themselves, too. Is this really happening? Are we truly this evenly matched, this obstinate and, under incredible pressure, performing so superlatively, inning after breathless inning?"

Kenley Jansen, the Dodgers' indomitable closer, was pitching for the fourth time in the World Series and the 11th time in the playoffs. In the bottom of the 10th, the analytic odds caught up with him. He hit a batter and walked another.

Bregman came to the plate. Those who know him have compared the young New Mexican to Johnny Manziel—without the self-destructive tendencies, they hasten to add. Manziel won the Heisman Trophy for his incredible exploits as quarterback for the Texas Aggies, before partying and alcohol cratered his career. Bregman is too smart and too responsible to allow something like that to happen to him, but like Manziel he's a superb athlete, just a little crazy and seemingly fearless. Facing Jansen in the fifth game of a World Series was exactly where he wanted to be.

"That guy lives for stuff like this," Springer told reporters after the game. "He loves it. I noticed he was digging in the box a little harder. He wanted to be the guy to do it."

Bregman had never had a walk-off hit in his career. The Dodgers held a meeting at the mound. Speedy Derek Fisher trotted out to second base to pinch run for McCann. Astros fans were screaming, clapping, twirling orange towels, stamping their feet. Every person in the park was standing, including overalls-clad train engineer Bobby Dynamite. Arms crossed, he was leaning against the vintage locomotive above left field. It had been a busy night.

"Springer had a huge at bat and walked right before me," Bregman said later. "I took one more swing on the on-deck circle, and I looked to Correa. Correa said, 'It's your time.'

"I thought, 'What's your approach going to be?' And I said, 'I saw him [Saturday] night and he threw me a slider, and [I] was fortunate enough to put a good swing on it and hit it out of the yard.' I basically eliminated the slider, and I said, 'I need to get a pitch that I can stay on top of, because he's a guy that throws high cutters, and a guy that gets a lot of fly-ball outs.'

"So I was looking for something down in the zone that I could stay on top of it."

Jansen's 92-mile-per-hour cutter sliced over the outer half of the plate. Bregman managed to get the barrel of his black, Louisiana-crafted Marucci bat on it, and finally, finally, after all the homers, comebacks, blown leads, and last-gasp rallies, this game was about to come to a glorious end. The rookie third baseman lined the pitch over the head of shortstop Seager and into left field.

With Fisher sprinting from second, Bregman was thinking as he rounded first there was no way left fielder Andre Ethier could throw the guy out. "As soon as it left the bat, I knew Fisher would score," he said. "He's probably the fastest guy in baseball."

It was one in the morning, and the irrepressible young Bregman screamed. "Aaaaaaiiieeee!" The train whistle blew, barely audible in the mayhem bouncing off the roof. Minute Maid was bedlam. Astros fans couldn't believe what they had just witnessed. No one else could either.

"Did it really happen?" ESPN's David Schoenfield wondered. "Sweet mother of all that's pure and good, this insanity most definitely did happen, as the 43,000-something fans in attendance at Minute Maid Park will tell their kids and their grandkids and their neighbors and the woman in line at the grocery store and the coworker at the office they haven't talked to in two years. Games like this bring us together. The entire city of Houston will be talking baseball on Monday morning."

"I can't tell you how many times I've said, 'This is the craziest game of my life,'" winning pitcher Musgrove told reporters. "This was the craziest game of my life."

Far from the noise in downtown Houston, a 97-year-old baseball fan whose diamond memories stretch back to Babe Ruth had something to say about a game he had stayed awake deep into the night to watch:

"Like other New York homies," the New Yorker's Roger Angell wrote, "I had adopted a sulky indifference when our young wildcard Yanks failed by one game in the League Championships, and only lately have I given full notice to this thrilling Astros bunch, not just the compact powerhouse Altuve but those surrounding him in the upper end of the lineup—the leadoff center-fielder Springer, the tall and beautifully athletic shortstop Correa, and the third-baseman Alex Bregman, my M.V.P. to date, whose clenched-jaw at-bats and key hits—his single scored the winning run on Sunday night—were matched only by his brilliant defensive plays at his corner. Not in the stats but also sweetly notable was the Astros' affection for one another and their boyish excitement over what they were watching and again making happen."

CHAPTER 13

Sweet '17

Screw it. We're going to Houston.

JUSTIN VERLANDER, 10 MINUTES BEFORE

A TRADE DEADLINE

Long-suffering Astros fans at Minute Maid Park never hauled out brown-paper-bag masks, even though they had to tolerate three seasons of triple-digit losses. To cap off the dismal 2013 season, the team lost 15 games in a row. As the 2014 season got under way, fans began to see glimmers of hope—despite a measly team payroll of $22 million (compared to $124 million in 2017) and a bad local TV deal that was draining revenues. Their Astros were becoming almost respectable.

The multitalented José Altuve broke through in 2014, leading the league in batting average, hits, and stolen bases. George Springer made his debut. Though his average was a career-low .231, he hit 20 home runs in just 295 at bats. Dallas Keuchel established himself as the ace of the pitching staff, and rookie pitcher Collin McHugh had a breakout season in the rotation.

The Astros finished 70–92, a 19–win improvement over '13.

They didn't make the playoffs, but the team avoided last place in the American League West, finishing three games ahead of their in-state rivals, the Texas Rangers, and that was noteworthy: it was the first time since 2010 that the Astros had not finished as division doormats.

Despite the improvement, Bo Porter, the Astros' rookie manager, lasted only two seasons. Jeff Luhnow fired him in '14 with just 24 games to go. Sports-talk radio bloviators, newspaper opinionators, and legions of bloggers spun theories about what went down: personality differences, bad communication, too much trust in analytics.

Ben Lindbergh of the now-defunct *Grantland* had a slightly different take, one that makes sense to me after talking to several people close to the situation. He noted that "the first-time skipper was asked to do something difficult: Lose more than any other major league manager." Sure, it was obvious what the Astros were doing, and, as Lindbergh noted, Luhnow had insisted in 2012 that the club would be competitive just as soon as possible, but it would be hard for anyone to wait years before wins became a bit more common. Porter landed a job with the Braves, while Jim Crane and company went looking for a manager who could tolerate waiting.

When the Astros gathered in Florida for spring training in 2015, they took the field for a skipper who seemed to embody everything that baseball analytics represented. There was nothing Stengelesque about Andrew Jay Hinch, nothing crusty or eccentric. Just over 40 at the time, Hinch was smart, articulate, and comfortable with the numbers game, but he also had enough on-field experience to be considered a baseball man. Born in Iowa, he had grown up in Oklahoma and had been an All-American catcher at Stanford University, where he majored in psychology.

"He's a very savvy communicator," a friend of his said. "He has an ease about him, plus he spends a lot of time with the media. I'm not sure his players realize how much he takes the heat off them by talking to the media himself."

He had what you might politely call an uneventful major league career, playing in the majors for eight years for four different teams and compiling an anemic .219 batting average. "When you don't hit a slider consistently, you're not going to play very long," he told reporters. "And there's only so far personality can take you as a backup catcher."

Despite having no experience as a manager or coach, Hinch was named manager of the Arizona Diamondbacks at age 34. It wasn't a good fit, in part because he inherited a staff of grizzled coaches—including Kirk Gibson, the iconic Dodgers slugger—who had resisted moving into the modern era.

Catchers with mediocre playing skills often make good managers; think Joe Girardi, formerly the Yankees' manager, or Bruce Bochy of the Giants. They're baseball's quarterbacks, after all; they know the game's intricacies. If they're grinders, not stars, they've had to work hard to learn the game, just to keep their precarious perch on a major league roster.

Hinch may have been a good manager, but the old catcher/young manager lost more often than he won at Phoenix. His .420 winning percentage over part of two seasons ranked as the second-lowest in Diamondbacks history. When Arizona fired him on July 1, 2010, the young baseball man went west, catching on as vice president of professional scouting for the San Diego Padres. He stayed four years before the Astros tapped him as manager.

Houston was a chance for a fresh start for Hinch, as it had been for many newcomers since the city's founding. Not only was he perceptive enough to learn from his desert sojourn managing the Diamondbacks, but also he joined the Astros just as Luhnow's dream was becoming reality.

"Hinch came along at the perfect time," *Houston Chronicle* columnist Brian Smith told me. "He has an analytics background, but he also understands how hard it is to play the game. He's the perfect blend of new and old."

The personable, young skipper soon became known as a players' manager, with some fine, young players to work with. At the same time, he could be a hard-ass when necessary, and his players trusted his judgment.

Reporters asked Keuchel about Hinch as the '15 Astros began postseason play against the New York Yankees. "He's been such a delight, especially in spring training, getting to know the guy," the young pitcher said. "Very open door, very transparent. It was refreshing."

"Belief has to come before performance," Hinch told the *Houston Chronicle*'s David Barron a couple of years later. "My job is to get the most out of players. We think coaching is yelling and berating. We think coaching is this physical altercation, 'you've got to get tougher.' It's not. Coaching is belief."

Hinch's disdain for the drill-sergeant mentality and his loyalty to the guys who played for him were admirable traits, but he also knew they had to throw pitches and hit baseballs. They had to win.

And they did. Altuve and Keuchel finally had some help, including a 20-year-old shortstop named Carlos Correa who joined the team in midseason. Keuchel compiled a perfect 15–0 record at Minute Maid.

The 2015 Astros won 86 games, clinched a wild-card berth and defeated the New York Yankees 3–0 in a one-game playoff at Yankee Stadium. It was their first appearance in the postseason since 2005.

In the best-of-five American League Division Series, the Astros took a 2–1 lead against the Kansas City Royals and were six outs away from closing it out at home. Going into the eighth inning of Game 4, trying to protect a 6–2 lead, reliever Will Harris gave up four hits in a row. Reliever Tony Sipp gave up another one. Rookie shortstop Correa mishandled a double-play grounder, and the lead evaporated like morning fog over nearby Buffalo Bayou. Royals 9, Astros 6.

Two days later, the Astros were flying home to Houston, cloud-watching out porthole windows and pondering what might have been. As ESPN's Scott Lauber tells the story, Altuve ended up in Hinch's office sobbing tears of frustration and disappointment.

"That was our first arrival, the first time we were really, in some ways, respected again in the game," Hinch told Lauber. "We had good players, good talent, and we won games. And we celebrated a couple of times. We went to Yankee Stadium and won the wild-card game. Those were all great memories for those guys, for guys like José who came through the lean years where we were losing and came out of it now feeling like a winner."

For Altuve, that wasn't enough. "I'm coming from a team that lost 100 games in a row three years, three straight years," he said. "Most of the guys inside the clubhouse in 2015, it was their first playoff. You don't know what to expect."

What Altuve expected was to be battling for a championship again in 2016. But that Astros goal got derailed. The team got off to a miserable 7–17 start in April, endured injuries to key players, and never found the momentum they needed. They went 84–78, finishing third in the American League West.

Keuchel suggested that the Astros were experiencing what I might describe as a form of baseball PTSD after coming so close and then losing to the Royals. As he pointed out, the Astros in '16 were pretty much the same formidable team they had been the season before, but they didn't get the same results.

"We were just some young group in '15 playing with a little swagger and some 'funness' to us," he told Lauber. "In '16, it was more of a job and a burden, and you can't win that way. We weren't in a position to win last year."

Luhnow realized his analytics mix needed a few more ingredients. Increasing revenues, a better TV deal, and Crane's willingness to dig a little deeper meant that team payroll was on an upward trajectory—from $22 million in 2013 to $69 million in '16, and $124 million in '17. With more money to play with, the GM and his operations department went looking for veteran leadership in the clubhouse. The Astros needed graybeards who knew, perhaps intuitively, how to keep their youngsters from being buffeted by despair when the going got tough—and to keep them from launching into a dangerous Icarian spiral when things went well.

Luhnow signed free agent Carlos Beltrán, a former Astro, to a one-year deal. At 40, the switch-hitting slugger (435 home runs) and future Hall of Fame candidate was a designated hitter exclusively; his new teammates dressed in black and held a mock funeral in the outfield for his glove. He had posted only a .776 OPS in a stint with the Texas Rangers in 2016, but his prowess at the plate, or lack thereof, was of secondary interest. Respected throughout baseball, he became, in essence, a player-coach and often counseled young Alex Bregman about hitting, about staying calm and collected. The Puerto Rican native became a mentor on the field and off for the Astros' numerous Latin American players.

The club also traded for catcher Brian McCann when the Yankees decided to go with the younger Gary Sanchez. McCann, a veteran who knew how to handle pitchers, could still hit and, like Beltrán, would be a steadying influence in the clubhouse. The club signed Josh Reddick to a four-year, $52 million contract. The fiery Southerner from Georgia was nobody's idea of a calming influence, but he had put together some good years in Oakland. Luhnow and the numbers guys believed he could still produce.

"I think that was huge for us," Correa told Lauber, alluding to the veterans Luhnow welcomed into the mix. "Last year, we had a young team with a lot of talent, but that leadership from a veteran guy we didn't have. And this year, with McCann, Beltrán, Reddick showing up, besides their baseball skills they are great guys in the clubhouse, and they taught us so much about the game, things that we didn't know about."

———————————

Everything clicked. For the first two months of the season, the daily headline on the front page of the *Houston Chronicle* sports section seemed stuck in happy *Groundhog Day* mode. Every day, it seemed, readers woke up to some version of "Astros Win."

The team was 38–16 through the end of May, and with 50 wins in 74 games—a club record—had just about wrapped up the division title before the All-Star break. A third of the way through the regular season, the winningest team in baseball was on a 114-win pace.

"We've been doing it for two months. We need to do it for four more months," Correa told reporters. "I think we're in a good position right now. But we're not going to get comfortable. We're going to strive for more."

Injuries to Keuchel, to Lance McCullers, and to Correa, who was out for six weeks with a torn thumb ligament, slowed them down a bit, but nobody came close to catching them.

And then the rains came and the devastating floods. Baseball suddenly became a secondary concern to a soggy, devastated city, and no one could predict how a young team would respond to the destruction and despair around them. The players weren't sure themselves. As Hinch put it, who could think about a child's game when thousands in your city had no place to live?

When an earthquake struck the Bay Area during the 1989 World Series, the baseball commissioner delayed the series for 10 days. The A's spent that time in Arizona, working out and keeping sharp away from the chaos and destruction back home. The Astros could have done something similar during their first couple of weeks after Harvey. The team could have stayed away, stayed focused on baseball while their city struggled to recover. The fans could have stayed away too. Neither happened in Houston.

"I know the city has been through a lot with the hurricane.

They are the biggest reason why we're here," Altuve would say on the eve of the World Series in LA. His teammates expressed similar sentiments. They stayed involved with their adopted city.

———————————

Five days after Harvey hit, with the city of Houston wounded and reeling, Luhnow was stuck in Los Angeles. He had been unable to get home after the Astros' series with the Angels because of the hurricane. As he sat at his impromptu office at the dining room table of his in-laws' Brentwood home, the Astros' GM considered the impending August 31 trade deadline. That was the last day teams could acquire players and have them eligible for any post-season play. The Astros were leading their division by a mile. Could they go all the way? Luhnow and the front office were about to send the strongest signal yet that they were going for broke in '17.

The GM and his field manager realized that the Astros needed one more quality starting pitcher, someone experienced, reliable, and effective, for the home stretch. With the deadline approaching, Luhnow also knew he still might have time to swing a deal for one of the best pitchers in baseball. He'd have to hurry.

Justin Verlander, a former MVP and a Cy Young Award winner, had been the Detroit Tigers' premier pitcher for more than a decade. The veteran right-hander figured he'd finish out his 13th major league season with the only team he'd ever pitched for, even as the Tigers would soon begin rebuilding and restocking with younger players. Verlander was 34, still strong and effective, but 34 nonetheless.

As Jake Kaplan, Astros beat writer for the *Houston Chronicle*, tells the story, Verlander had no idea that on August 31, 2017, he would have to make the hardest decision of his baseball life, almost immediately. He told Kaplan he didn't like making decisions rashly, but when the Astros came courting on deadline, he had no choice.

"So I just never really thought about it," he told Kaplan. "That was my only way to continue to go about my job in Detroit. If I'm going to heavily think about [trade possibilities], then I'm not going to be doing my job on the mound. It was just kind of background noise until all of a sudden."

The Astros front office had looked at Verlander earlier in the summer, among several other top-of-the-line pitchers they were considering before a July 31 trade deadline. They almost swung a deal for Zack Britton of the Orioles, but the Birds backed out at the last minute. They talked about Yu Darvish, who left the Rangers for the Dodgers on July 31. Verlander was always their first choice, Crane has said.

August 31 was a Thursday, and Verlander was at home in his apartment in the Detroit suburb of Birmingham. The Tigers were off. He had pitched the day before, throwing six innings of one-run game against the Colorado Rockies at Coors Field in Denver. That afternoon, he began to notice on social media that the Tigers were prowling in the trade jungle. He saw that the team had shipped All-Star outfielder Jason Upton to the Los Angeles Angels. Knowing that he himself had been a topic of discussion for at least a month, he texted Tigers GM Al Avila to see if his name might be coming up again. Avila told him talks were ongoing but no deal was probable.

If Verlander wasn't traded before 11:00 p.m., Central Standard Time, he would finish out the season in Bobby Bare's Dee-troit City.

Luhnow had talked to Avila about Verlander before the July 31 non-waiver trade deadline, but when nothing happened, the bloggers and the social media mavens had gotten after him for not pulling off a significant deal.

From the dining-room-table office in Brentwood, Luhnow already had made a Thursday-morning trade for Cameron Maybin of the Angels, once he met the Angels' demand that the Astros assume the roughly $1.5 million left on the outfielder's $9 million salary for the '17 season. What the Astros GM didn't know at the time was that he was involved in a tripartite Rubix Cube maneuver. The Angels had agreed to part with Maybin (twist the cube), because they had acquired Upton from the Tigers (twist it again), and that deal would help facilitate the Verlander trade (and again).

"I woke up probably pretty pessimistic that anything would happen," Luhnow told Kaplan. "At one point early in the morning California time, I became much more optimistic. Then it waned again, and I became pessimistic. That cycle continued about every couple of hours, and sometimes there were just minutes between cycles. It was pretty intense."

"It was agonizing not knowing," Hinch told reporters. "I texted back and forth, made phone calls back and forth with Jeff, and it was on, it was off, it was on, it was off. I tried not to follow social media, because that's the death trap for managers."

At 6:00 p.m. Pacific Time, Luhnow found himself, strangely enough, at the *Bad News Bears Field* in West LA, where he had promised his 11-year-old nephew he would watch his Little League team practice. (Baseball fans who grew up in the '70s will remember, apropos of nothing, that the beloved Bad News Bears traveled to Houston to play in the 1977 movie sequel, *The Bad News Bears in Breaking Training*.) His nephew's coach asked Luhnow to say a few words to the team—unaware that the Astros GM was trying to negotiate one of the biggest trades in Astros history.

The clock was ticking, and the two GMs were talking money. Kaplan was able to find out from people unable to speak publicly that the Astros earlier in August had offered to pay $18 million annually of the $28 million Verlander will make in 2018 and 2019. That was $2 million below Detroit's asking price.

The Astros later gave in and agreed to pay $19 million per year. The deal Luhnow and Avila were close to concluding would send the highly touted 19-year-old right-hander Franklin Perez, outfielder Daz Cameron, and catcher Jake Rogers to Detroit in exchange for Verlander. Key to the deal was Crane's approval to spend more on Verlander ($40 million) than the team's entire payroll ($13 million) from just four seasons earlier.

Luhnow was back at his in-laws' house getting ready for dinner out—his wife, Gina, had made an 8:15 reservation—when he and Avila agreed they had a done deal. But what about Verlander himself? The pitcher had full no-trade rights and could very well decide to quash the deal. Luhnow asked his wife to push their dinner reservation to 9:00 or 9:15 p.m. Pacific. That would be 11:15 Central—45 minutes to deadline.

Back in Michigan, Verlander and his fiancée, the supermodel Kate Upton, had gone for a late dinner, still not expecting a trade. Walking home from the restaurant at about 11:20 p.m., Eastern, Verlander's phone rang. It was Avila.

"And then I had to make the hardest decision I've ever had to make in baseball," Verlander told Kaplan.

Back at the apartment, Verlander was pacing back and forth and making calls, many to his agent. If he had to leave Detroit, he had been hoping to join either the Cubs or Dodgers. (He and Upton have a home in LA.) He knew little about Houston, other than the distressing scenes of flood devastation he'd been seeing on the news.

"Given that period of time, I just wanted to get as much information as I could, whatever it was," he told Kaplan. "'What are we talking about in two years? What are we talking about right now? What's the locker room like? What are these guys like? What's the town like?...There was just a hurricane there. Obviously, they're in bad shape as a city. What's that like? Can I live somewhere?' Stuff I hadn't even thought of. I was just trying to weigh all of that."

He took a call from Keuchel, the man who would be his co-ace if he decided to make the move. The Astros' mound mainstay was at home in Houston, having landed earlier in the evening from St. Petersburg, Florida, where the Astros has played their three "home" games against the Mets. Keuchel, among those who had complained when the Astros failed to make a significant trade a month earlier, told Verlander he was hearing rumors.

Keuchel told the *Chronicle*'s Kaplan the gist of his conversation went something like: "'Hey, I'm not trying to take too much of your time up. You won't regret your decision to come here. Obviously, your window for winning in Detroit is damn near closed, and ours is wide open.'

"I figured the only thing left in his legacy is to win a World Series, because he's pretty much done everything else," Keuchel told Kaplan. "I was hoping that would resonate in his mind rather quickly, and I think it did."

Verlander told Kaplan he didn't remember the exact time he made the decision to accept the trade. It couldn't have been much earlier than 11:50 p.m. Eastern, 10 minutes until the deadline, he said.

"I knew in my brain that I had all of the information. I had everything that I was going to have," he said. "I'm not exactly sure what time it was, but it was late, and in the middle of one of my paces I look at Kate and go, 'Screw it. We're going to Houston.' And she goes, 'OK!' and got excited. It was a pretty cool moment, really."

Luhnow was on his way to dinner, his wife driving. At about 9:15 p.m. Pacific time, 15 minutes after the deadline, he got the call. Justin Verlander was headed to Houston.

———————

"Whether Crane took out his checkbook and spent because his devastated hometown desperately needed a lift, or because he felt he had to live up to his promise, or because he simply believed in his general manager's analysis, only time will fully reveal," the *Chronicle*'s Barron mused. "Whatever the answer, it was a promise kept and a plan fulfilled. And if the formula holds, there may be more titles to come."

It was immediately obvious that Crane would get his money's worth from his newest acquisition. Verlander's impact was almost instantaneous. The way he carried himself, the easy, natural way he interacted with his new teammates and the respect they obviously had for him, the way he approached his profession—they all made an impression. He inspired the Astros, including Keuchel, to up their game. He would join Beltrán and McCann as a mentor to the younger players. They took to him immediately.

On the mound he would provide pitching reliability beyond Keuchel and McCullers. Keuchel had started the season looking like his Cy Young self before losing two months to injury, and McCullers, who had made only four starts since the All-Star break, had not regained his form. The Astros needed a pitching spark. For the rest of the season, however long it lasted, the newcomer likely would be the ace.

Verlander got to Houston on Saturday, September 2—five weeks left in the regular season—and showed up at Minute Maid that afternoon during the first game of a doubleheader. Between games, he threw in the bullpen. His new teammates stopped to watch the smooth, classic delivery. They heard the ball pop when it hit the catcher's mitt.

When El Grande, the center field jumbotron, briefly showed him in the Astros dugout, fans stood and roared. They were excited. Players were excited. Verlander was excited, a long-time baseball reporter told me. "I knew immediately this was a grown-up pitcher," she said.

What a time to arrive! A couple of weeks after Verlander traded in his Tigers' old-English "D" cap for one featuring an orange star and block "H," the Astros won their first division title since 2001, during the Craig Biggio–Jeff Bagwell era. The title clicked into place with an Astros win over the Seattle Mariners and a loss by the Los Angeles Angels.

Making his home debut against the Mariners after two appearances on the road, Verlander pitched seven strong innings: he allowed three hits and a run, walking one and striking out 10. He faced only two batters over the minimum. Through September, he was 5–0, with an earned run average of 1.06.

Clinching the AL West in their 149th game of the season, the team's second postseason appearance in three seasons validated the long, hard years in the wilderness and the slow, patient rebuilding job that Luhnow orchestrated.

"We wanted to do it in front of our home fans," Keuchel told reporters. "I had been joking before that the clubhouse (attendants) wanted us to do it on the road, because they didn't want us to trash the clubhouse. But to clinch in front of our home fans, who have supported us the last couple of years as we've gotten better and better, it just means the world. We're hoping to lock up some home field advantage as well, so we can get some more home crowds behind us."

On the 5th of October, that's exactly what they got—and more. The AL East champion Boston Red Sox came to town and had to listen to 43,000-plus Astros fans serenade Altuve with booming chants of "MVP, MVP" each time he came to the plate. The Red Sox may have been chanting under their breath along with them after Altuve's night was done. In his team's 8–2 win, the five-time All-Star and American League batting champ became the ninth player in major league history to hit three home runs in a postseason game.

The first two were shots off Boston left-hander Chris Sale, a six-time All-Star. The third, off rookie right-hander Austin Maddox, left fans, and teammates, in awe.

"That was amazing to watch," said Correa, who hits behind Altuve in the Astros order. "He made me feel like a leadoff hitter today."

"He's a joke," Springer said. "He said he's never hit three homers in a game in his life. That's a great day to hit three. The dude's a 'create a player.' He's the MVP of the league. I don't see who else could be. He's unbelievable."

Verlander was on the mound for the Astros. He didn't have his best stuff, but it was good enough to get him through six innings while giving up only two runs. He struck out only three and walked two.

The next night, still in Houston, Correa picked up where Altuve left off. He launched a two-run homer off Boston's Drew Pomeranz in the first inning and then broke open the game with a two-run double off Addison Reed in the sixth. It was the young shortstop's second career four-RBI postseason game, after Game 4 of the 2015 ALDS.

Keuchel gave the Astros six solid innings, retiring 13 consecutive batters between the second and the sixth. He allowed only one run in another 8–2 victory for the Astros.

The Astros took their 2–0 advantage to Boston, where, unlike in Houston, there really was an autumn. Orange and yellow leaves were falling, and in the first game at venerable Fenway Park, so were the visitors from the Lone Star State. The Red Sox broke open a tight game with a six-run seventh inning, all the cushion former

Cy Young winner David Price needed as he quieted the Astros' hot bats during four innings of scoreless relief. The Astros' bullpen was charged with 7 of Boston's 10 runs. Red Sox 10, Astros 3.

"We're going to be fine," Hinch said when it was over. "We'll bounce back out of this and come back and play hard. But this is playoff baseball. If anybody thought the Red Sox were going to lay down, probably rethink it."

Hinch was right; Game 4 wasn't easy. When Andrew Benintendi smashed a two-run homer off Verlander, pitching in relief in the fifth inning, momentum seemed to shift toward the home team. His round-tripper put the Red Sox ahead 3–2.

Sale, also pitching in relief, had dominated the Astros for four consecutive innings, allowing only two hits and striking out six without issuing a walk. He had relied on sliders and a 99-mile-per-hour fastball, but when Bregman led off the eighth inning for the Astros, the Red Sox pitcher resorted to changeups. The young third baseman was ready, and when Sale made a mistake on one, he delivered the biggest hit of his brief career, a solo blast over the Green Monster in left field, tying the score at 4.

Later in the inning, Evan Gattis reached first on a single, and Maybin came in to run for him. With Springer coming to the plate, Sale gave way to Boston's premier closer, Craig Kimbrel, who walked Springer. To the plate came Reddick, who fouled off four pitches before lacing into a 99-mile-per-hour fastball that he drove the other way into left field. Maybin scored from second. Astros 4, Red Sox 3.

Astros reliever Ken Giles shut down the Red Sox in the bottom of the eighth. In the top of the ninth, with runners at first and second, pinch hitter Beltrán bounced a curveball off the Green

Monster for a run-scoring double. That insurance run loomed large when Giles gave up an inside-the-park home run to Rafael Devers in the bottom of the ninth. The Astros reliever recovered to shut down the last three hitters, setting the stage for shouts and hugs and spewed bottles of Korbel bubbly in the clubhouse.

"It's a little bit like a redemption feeling," McCullers told reporters, expressing what many of his teammates no doubt were feeling as Giles battled through the eighth and ninth innings. "We were six outs away in '15, man. We were six outs away from the ALCS. The team that beat us [the Kansas City Royals] ended up winning the World Series. It was tough for everyone. It's still been tough for everybody. So just to close it out and to go in the ALCS and give the fans this time to enjoy, it's pretty cool."

———————

The Astros have played the New York Yankees many times since that long-ago afternoon when Mickey Mantle hit the first home run in the Astrodome. Still, the Yankees were the Yankees. Whenever they came to town—actually any town—they carried with them the aura of Babe Ruth and Lou Gehrig, Mickey Mantle and Roger Maris, and, more recently, Derek Jeter and Alex Rodriguez, not to mention the many championships the Bronx Bombers have amassed over the years.

In 2017, they came to town with yet another legend in the making—a six-foot-seven-inch rookie who had hit 52 home runs during the regular season and who was Altuve's chief rival for MVP. Young Aaron Judge had the potential to make fans forget the Babe—unless, that is, he had to face Keuchel regularly. The bearded left-hander's career numbers against the Yankees in eight starts include a 1.09 ERA. In 57⅔ innings against the Yankees, he has never allowed a home run. Against Keuchel in Game 1 of the American League Championship Series, the Astros' first in 12 years, Keuchel allowed the Yankees' young giant a meaningless single. Nothing else.

The Astros' superb starter pitched seven scoreless innings against a Yankees lineup that had produced the second-most runs in the majors during the regular season. He gave up only four hits—all singles—and struck out 10.

"When the sinker is moving and the gun is hitting 90, I know he's going to be lights out," Correa said.

The Astros managed to score two runs off the Yankees' Masahiro Tanaka, who pitched masterfully himself. The runs came on hits from Altuve, Correa, and Marwin Gonzalez.

Gonzalez, an infielder playing left field, saved a run for Keuchel in the fifth inning when he fielded Judge's single and fired a strike to home plate to get Greg Bird, who was trying to score from second.

"You can't really say enough about the play of Marwin the whole season," Keuchel said. "He's literally the most undervalued player in the big leagues. And now that we got national attention, we're seeing everybody's worth."

Astros 2, Yankees 1. With superb pitching and timely defense, the home team overruled a Judge.

In Game 2, also at home, the Astros relied on the same ingredients and got the same score, 2–1. This time it was Verlander, doing exactly what the Astros envisioned when he had said yes six weeks earlier. Against the Yankees on October 13, he set a career playoff high with 13 strikeouts, while giving up only five hits and one earned run in nine strong innings. The Astros crowd was enraptured. They expressed themselves in one long, continuous roar.

"That was probably the loudest I heard a ballpark or close to it. And I've been part of some pretty loud moments," Verlander said afterward. "The way those fans were pushing me to finish that game—or finish the ninth inning and have a chance to win the game—I mean, that matters. It gets your adrenaline going."

With the score tied at 1 in the bottom of the ninth, Altuve slapped a single and Correa followed with a liner to right-center. Third base coach Gary Pettis frantically waved the speedy Altuve home. The ball beat him to the plate, he slid, the umpire spread his arms parallel to the ground as he shouted "Safe!" and there were the jubilant Astros bounding out of the dugout to greet their amazing MVP (made official a few weeks later).

Two games to zero. Had the Astros finally beaten the lingering Royals hex? Only time and how they fared in fabled Yankee Stadium would tell the tale.

Game 3 of that tale did not have a happy ending for the guys from Space City. Starter Charlie Morton surrendered to a couple of two-out rallies, including a three-run homer by Ruth-to-be Judge. Left fielder Maybin misplayed a fly ball down the line, costing Morton an out and eventually four runs, including Judge's homer. Catcher Gattis failed to block a Morton curveball in the dirt with a runner on third base.

The Yankees veteran left-hander CC Sabathia and reliever Adam Warren silenced Astros' bats. American League batting champion Altuve was 0-for-4. A bases-loaded walk to Bregman in the ninth accounted for the Astros' only run. They left 11 runners on base. Yankees 8, Astros 1. Series 2–1 Astros.

In Game 4, still in New York, the Astros were leading 4–2 after seven innings. The lead put them six outs away from needing only one more win to clinch the franchise's second World Series appearance. A Game 4 victory would put Yankee-tamer Keuchel on the mound at Yankee Stadium to close it out in Game 5.

Didn't happen. McCullers pitched well, except for a towering home run Judge hit to center field, but the bullpen couldn't hold and the Astros couldn't hit. The best offense in the major leagues was hitting a pathetic .153 through four games with the Yankees, with only six extra-base hits in 118 at bats.

"We have to keep fighting," designated hitter Beltrán said after the 6–4 Yankees victory. "It wasn't going to be easy."

The next night, still in the rebuilt House That Ruth Built, it got harder. With Yankees starter Tanaka on the mound for seven innings and reliever Tommy Kahnle finishing up, the Astros still couldn't hit. Shut out for the first time in the playoffs since the final game of the 2005 World Series, the Astros managed only four hits, a day after getting a measly three. Against the Yankees Reddick was 0-for-17, Springer 2-for-18, Bregman 2-for-17.

In the visitors' clubhouse after the game, Beltrán and McCann held a team meeting. The two veterans didn't need to remind their downcast teammates that they were on the brink of elimination after coming so far. They didn't need to mention that the wild-card Yanks, the upstart Yanks, were one win away from the World Series, one win away from eliminating a team that had won 101 regular-season games, a team that saw the Series as its destiny.

"The message was that we cannot feel sorry about ourselves,"

Beltrán said. "We won the first two games, we lost the three games here, and now we're going to have the opportunity to go home and try to do what they did here. Win the next two games and try to move on to the next round. That's the mentality."

Beltrán didn't mention Kansas City, 2015.

CHAPTER 14

Houston in Recovery

There were so many people who were so amazing.

ASTROS FAN JIM DEAN

T he stumbling Astros were coming home from New York to a city that still believed, even as many fans continued to grapple with the headaches and heartaches that lingered weeks after Harvey. The Pearland house where Jim and Jennifer Dean and their family lived, inundated by at least 10 inches of floodwater, was still a sodden mess. When Jim got back to the house a couple of days after he and his family evacuated in a boat, an inch of fetid water remained inside.

It was a depressing experience but certainly not an uncommon one. Richard Murray, a well-known professor of political science at the University of Houston, had to flee his home near Brays Bayou, a house he had owned since 1978, to a neighbor's home on higher ground. A TV crew with a boat later ferried the 77-year-old professor—along with Marco, his big, lumbering Spinone Italiano—out of his flooded neighborhood to a nearby grocery store parking lot, where his son, Kier Murray, picked him up. The elder Murray and his dog lived for weeks with his son, daughter-in-law, and their two youngsters. Like so many Houstonians, he spent hours every day cleaning up and waiting for crews to basically rebuild the house.

The neighborhood near the bayou, Kier Murray said, "was on the front end of a rolling disaster."

When Harvey hit, Murray's wife, Debbie Hartman, was in the couple's summer home in the pine-covered hills above northern California's Napa Valley. With her was her elderly mother, Doris Embry, who is disabled. While Murray dealt with the aftermath of Harvey, the two women had their own natural disaster to cope with. Raging wildfires, the flames limning the rim of hills above their home, forced them to evacuate to a friend's house in nearby Yountville and then to a motel. It would be weeks before they got back to Houston—to a home still in a state of repair.

In the Houston suburb of Spring, concert pianist and Prairie View A&M University dean Danny Kelley, 70, along with his wife, Denise, a physician, were forced out of their home. I had met Kelley long, long ago, when he was a five-year-old piano prodigy in the little Central Texas town of Cameron where he grew up. (Cameron also is the hometown of former Astros owner Drayton McLane Jr.) Back then, neighbors white and black were proud of the little African American kid with preternatural musical talent, and through the years he had gone back home occasionally to perform for special events. As he prepared for a major concert in New York City, Harvey claimed the Kelley family home and his Steinway grand piano, circa 1902.

More than 311,000 residences in Houston alone were either

damaged or destroyed. Thousands more beyond the city were made unlivable. A few weeks after Harvey, the *Chronicle* dispatched me on a drive down the Texas coast to assess the damage in the little beach communities, their plight overshadowed in the public eye by what had befallen Houston. The massive destruction I saw prompted a tinge of survivor's guilt, since Laura and I had been spared any damage back home, even though we live only a few blocks from Buffalo Bayou.

When I got out of my car to talk to people in Port Aransas, the smell of dead fish was almost overwhelming. Bloodthirsty mosquitoes zeroed in on my face and arms. As I took notes while interviewing local resident Flora Caylor Buerger, she brushed a sucking monster off my cheek and offered bug spray. She and husband John were proprietors of Angler's Court, seven frame cabins her grandfather had built in the late 1940s a few blocks from the beach. All seven remained standing after Harvey hit but were heavily damaged.

"I've been through Celia, Carla, but this is nothing like I've experienced," she told me. The Buergers were already making repairs, hoping to be ready for the influx of Winter Texans in the fall. If there was to be an influx.

The Buergers, the Kelleys, Dick Murray and Debbie Hartman— most every Harvey survivor you talk to—consider themselves fortunate. They had their difficulties, but they knew others with problems much more formidable than theirs. "Things, you can replace," Murray said, taking a break from lugging water-logged papers, books, and memorabilia to the curb from his flooded-out garage.

Jim Dean, 46, felt the same way, even though he, like thousands of other Houston-area residents, was "freaking out" at the enormity of the task he and wife Jennifer faced: trying to figure out how to repair a flooded home and get back to normal. With home insurance and flood insurance, the Deans realized they were among the "fortunate," but normal was a long way off.

The first step on a long trek was photographing the house. Next, he and friends plunged into the laborious task of ripping up carpet and padding, cutting out four feet of drywall, and dumping the stinking mess of debris in an empty lot next door. In the Deans' neighborhood and throughout the region, depressing, foul-smelling mounds of debris piled up; it took weeks for crews to haul them off.

"I lost track of time," Jim Dean said.

"I think everyone in Houston was like walking zombies," Jennifer Dean added.

Relatives, friends, and strangers all came by to help. People brought food. Others took flood-soaked clothes and towels home to launder and fold, a scene that played out in countless water-ravaged homes across the region. People walked through the neighborhood offering water and snacks. The Deans befriended neighbors they didn't know before the storm. They helped each other.

"There were so many people who were so amazing," Jim Dean said. Early on, daughter Haleigh's mother—Jennifer is her stepmom—drove in from her home near Baton Rouge, Louisiana, just to drop off food, returning home the same day. Their son Hudson's two teachers came by unannounced to check on him and his family and see if they could help. When Jim Dean joked he would like some tacos, the teachers happily obliged. A friend from Austin, nearly 200 miles away, dropped by with supplies. Haleigh spray-painted a large piece of cardboard with the words "God Bless Texas" and planted it in the muddy front yard to lift spirits around the neighborhood.

The Friday after their home flooded, the Deans moved into a one-bedroom motorhome Jennifer's parents drove over and parked in the driveway. The tedious work on the house continued: removing more debris, fighting to get the insurance money, throwing out treasured mementos. They were grateful to have the motorhome and were reluctant to complain, but it was so small.

Their house was uninhabitable, with all the appliances trashed, the water-soaked furniture ruined. Ah, but they still had power. And the 50-inch TV still worked. Jim Dean had his ice chest full of beer. And the Astros were still winning. The Deans needed a distraction, a really good one.

Jim Dean grew up watching the Astros, good teams and bad. He saw many a game at the Astrodome, and he went to school in nearby Alvin, Texas, with team president Reid Ryan, son of Nolan.

A laid-back guy with a quick smile and a full beard and mustache, Dean pretty much always wears a baseball cap, invariably one of his many Astros caps.

The Deans continued watching the Astros in their gutted-out home, sitting on camp chairs planted on the concrete floor. They had tried watching in the motorhome, but it just wasn't as comfortable. And, hey, they were superstitious; they were baseball fans, after all. Since they had been watching the team in the house when the Astros started winning, they didn't want to tempt fate by changing their TV-watching locale.

"We would always have the games on," Jim Dean said.

The season ended and the Astros stormed into the playoffs, with the Deans, like thousands of other Houstonians, still Harveyed out of their ravaged home.

Dean had an additional thought about this particular team and its response to Houston's adversity: "The Astros showed what Texas Strong is."

As a lifelong fan, Jim Dean had loved many Astros teams, but this lineup was special. "You watch these guys and how they play for the love of the game. They aren't the highest-paid, and some of them came to the U.S. with hardly anything. They suck you into the game and you get lost in it," he said. "We were relying on them to show the world something good was going to happen out of all of this."

For Dean, it was especially gratifying to watch the Astros beat the Yankees before taking on the Dodgers. "I didn't have to think about what I had to worry about the next day," he recalled (until the Yankees started taking Big Apple bites out of the visiting Astros).

Jennifer Dean suggested that the Astros, win or lose, were a unifying force for all of Houston.

The game-watching in the gutted house had become a ritual within a ritual, so much so that a friend told Jim Dean about how the Houston Chronicle was asking for Astros fan/Harvey victims to email them with details about how they were watching the World Series. Dean responded, and the next day, reporter Emily Foxhall called, talked to him about his family's Harvey experiences and asked if a photographer could come while he was watching the next game.

It was Game 6, two days after the Astros' sensational, heart-stopping 13–12 victory at home. The series was back in LA, and

Houston fans were ready for one more win to take the World Series on Halloween night.

Chronicle photographer Steve Gonzales came to the Deans' Harvey-damaged home for the game and stayed for about two and a half innings. The photo he took was named ESPN's photo of the year. (Jim Dean is sure the photo Gonzales snapped was at the moment George Springer committed an outfield error that Astros fans feared at the time would be costly.)

"It [the photo] looks depressing but we're not hurting. We're just waiting," Jennifer Dean said.

The iconic image prompted some online criticism, as well—speculation that the Deans had spent FEMA money on a new TV. They hadn't. Someone even remarked that they had an expensive Yeti cooler. They didn't.

———————

That's exactly what the Deans had been doing a few weeks earlier, when their hometown heroes, facing the fate of the dodo and the carrier pigeon—extinction—got ready to battle the Yankees at home. It wouldn't be the Alamo (to switch metaphors); that's the battle the Texans lost. They were determined to make it San Jacinto, the iconic battlefield a few miles from Minute Maid Park where Sam Houston and his ragtag army won a victory for the ages. (At least, that's what Astros fans with a yen for Texas history surely must have been thinking.)

The Astros' modern-day Sam Houston in Game 6 was a Virginia native, newly arrived from Michigan, a fellow named Justin Verlander. The tall, powerful right-hander gave up just five hits and one walk. He threw 99 pitches for 70 strikes in his seven-inning stint. He gave up just one run, a homer to Aaron Judge. He was in control from the first pitch on.

"He's been everything that we could have hoped for and more," manager A. J. Hinch said afterward. "This guy prepares. He rises to the moment."

Meanwhile, the Astros' bats rose up as well. José Altuve went 2-for-4 with three RBIs and his fourth home run of the postseason. Carlos Correa and Yuli Gurriel responded to Judge's solo homer in the eighth inning with back-to-back hits. The Astros pounded Yankees pitchers for seven runs.

The story, though, was the team's newcomer. "These Astros are hosting a Game 7," *Chronicle* columnist Brian T. Smith wrote. "They're alive in 2017 because of Verlander."

On a Saturday night in downtown Houston, they stayed alive, gloriously alive. When the night came to its raucous end, the Houston Astros had defeated the New York Yankees, had driven a stake through a Kansas City hex, had lifted up a city brought low by the devastation of Hurricane Harvey. The Houston Astros were American League champions.

The Astros' 4–0 victory in the seventh game of the championship series featured several heroes, including Charlie Morton, who threw five scoreless innings, and Lance McCullers Jr., who pitched the final four in relief.

"We had to make a decision on which guy was going to start, which guy was going to relieve," Hinch told reporters afterward. "We knew we were going to use both of them. I didn't know they were going to split the game and get us all 27 outs."

Evan Gattis got the Astros' Saturday-night hitting fever going when veteran left-hander CC Sabathia hung a slider and the Astros' DH slapped it over the left field wall. Catcher Brian McCann helped to beat his former teammates with a double to the right field corner. He had done the same thing the night before. His hit gave the Astros their final 4–0 lead.

The team's hero of heroes, the guy who's been the Astros' heart and soul and their best player through bad times and good, slapped one over the fence as well. Altuve's five postseason homers were the second most for an Astros player in a single postseason, trailing only teammate Carlos Beltrán, who had eight in 2004. A roaring, boisterous crowd, on their feet the whole game, showed Altuve their appreciation. So did Hinch.

"He is the Houston Astros right now," he said. "The way he's played, what he's persevered through, the teams he's been on, and yet he's still hungry. He's not going to be satisfied with that home run. And that's what I love about him."

In the top of the ninth, the crowd could pretty much tell what was about to happen. McCullers stuck out Didi Gregorius. He struck out Gary Sanchez. He got Greg Bird on a puny little pop-up. And then he threw his arms into the air as Minute Maid Park exploded. The Houston Astros had won the pennant.

CHAPTER 15

Dream Deferred

SERIES TIED, 3-3

Who can guarantee that you're going to be in Game 7 ever again?

ASTROS MANAGER A. J. HINCH

Ten days after the Astros were crowned American League champions and two days after they had taken a one-game lead in the World Series, Astros fans were hoping to see their heroes close it out. No more waiting. After heart-stopping Game 5, one of the wildest in Series history, they'd had enough drama to at least last the winter.

"I wanted it to be easy, anticlimactic," lifelong Astros fan David Fahrenthold said.

Maya Wadler had become such a huge Astros fan in the weeks after her family was flooded out of their home that she and her mom ventured to Minute Maid Park to watch Game 6 on the giant TV. "We needed it," she said.

In Sugar Land, the Dean family also anticipated one more exciting game and then a long winter ahead of reconstruction and repair, of slowly getting back to normal after an unbelievable year.

In their house taken down to the studs, they had the TV on, ready to see their Astros win a World Series.

As the Astros took batting practice at Dodger Stadium, the organist played the old chestnut, "Hotel California" ("This could be Heaven, or this could be Hell"), an appropriate ditty for Halloween night. The temperature at game time was football-weather 67 degrees, more than 30 degrees cooler than the scorching Series opener. Heavy clouds obscured the San Gabriels, and a shower fell during the middle innings.

Many baseball fans around the country were still getting to know the Astros, and as the Series progressed social media seemed to focus more and more on the club's young third baseman. Who is this guy who keeps making sterling defensive plays? Who keeps coming up with the key hit. Who is Alex Bregman?

If Jeff Luhnow was the quintessential moneyball baseball executive, Bregman was the quintessential moneyball player. He was scouted, assessed, seasoned in the minors, and then slotted into the exact spot where he could most help a team that trusted the odds.

Bregman grew up in Albuquerque, New Mexico, in a politically active family with a baseball pedigree. His parents are lawyers, and his father, Sam, has been the chairman of the state's Democratic Party. His grandfather served as general counsel for the Washington Senators in the 1960s and was instrumental in the move that brought the franchise to Dallas–Fort Worth, where the Senators became the Texas Rangers. Both his father and an uncle played baseball at the University of New Mexico.

Albuquerque's not exactly known as a baseball hotbed, but it boasts a venerable diamond tradition. Longtime fans of the Albuquerque Dukes, for many years a Dodgers farm team in the Pacific Coast League, recall the cool air of a summer evening, the starry skies, and good baseball. (The team is now known, I regret to say, as the Isotopes.)

Albuquerque was good for Bregman as well. When he was a 16-year-old sophomore at Albuquerque Academy, a private school with a superb baseball program, he was named USA Baseball Player of the Year. He expected to be drafted out of high school, but hurt his hand and missed his senior season. He accepted a scholarship to baseball powerhouse LSU, where school officials threatened to take away his key to the building that housed the batting cage, because he was in there all hours of the day and night.

"Obviously it's in his DNA," A. J. Hinch said after Bregman's Sunday heroics. "Since the day he showed up in the big leagues, he's had a great youthful exuberance about himself and confidence about himself that is unwavered."

"He's been supremely confident since the day he walked into a major league clubhouse," Astros broadcaster Steve Sparks told me. "I think he believes he'll hit .400 one day."

Bregman is one of eight players 23 years or younger who have hit multiple homers in the same World Series, joining such luminaries as Hank Aaron, Mickey Mantle, and Jimmie Foxx. That's some level.

The Astros knew from the beginning they had something special. They took him second overall in the 2015 draft. He was a shortstop at LSU, but with Correa installed at short, Bregman moved over to third and made the transition seamlessly.

The Astros brought him up in the middle of the 2016 season, and for much of the year he was the subject of trade rumors. The team needed pitching, and Bregman, despite his potential, might be expendable. Besides, he wasn't playing his natural position with the Astros. Nothing ever came of the rumors, particularly after his solid regular season in 2017—a .284 batting average with 19 homers, 71 RBIs, and an .827 on-base plus slugging percentage. His superlative performance in the World Series meant that he— along with George Springer, José Altuve, and Carlos Correa—had ascended to the untradeable.

Bregman, listed as six feet tall but likely a bit shorter, plays with a down-in-the-dirt grittiness that Justin Verlander said reminded him of Dustin Pedroia, the tough little second baseman for the Boston Red Sox. Verlander has seen him race after pop-ups, smash into the left field railing, as he did earlier in the AL Division Series with the Red Sox. He's seen him stand in against the game's hardest throwers.

"He's not scared at all," the veteran pitcher said. "I think you can see in some of the defensive plays he's made and some of the home runs he's hit against the pitchers that he hit them against, he thrives in big moments. When the pressure is on, he's a guy you want in your corner."

"You're talking about a 23-year-old kid who plays like a 30-year-old veteran," Altuve told reporters before Game 5. "He hits homers, he steals bases. I remember when I was 23 and I wasn't as good as him, so I feel like he's going to be a superstar."

In the first inning of Game 6, that Halloween Tuesday night, Bregman came to the plate after Springer had stuck out on four pitches and got the first hit of the game, lining a single to left field off Dodgers starter Rich Hill. He was left stranded when Altuve struck out and Correa ground out.

The Astros were looking to Verlander to end the Series in six, to go back to the Bayou City in triumph. They needed him to go as many innings as he could, since the bullpen had been unreliable throughout the postseason. With Verlander 9 and 0 since coming over from Detroit and MVP in the American League Championship Series, their confidence wasn't misplaced.

Before the game, reporters asked Hinch about Verlander's value to the team. "He's been big," the manager said. "I think the day we got him, there was an emotional tie to the city, because we were coming back from the hurricane, being relocated. There's something different when you put a major piece like that in your clubhouse. And I think his presence alone gave guys hope and belief that things were going to be good for us. We had two months left in the season. We hadn't won the division or hadn't done anything yet. But I think his demeanor, his preparation, his personality, his performance, all raised the bar for the organization."

For the first five innings, Verlander was unhittable. Hill was just as effective into the third, retiring seven straight batters. He also found time to allow Dodgers fans to indulge their animus toward Yuli Gurriel, the first time they'd seen him in person since the Yu Darvish incident in Houston during Game 3. With Gurriel set in the batter's box, Hill twice stepped off the mound and dallied longer than usual. Hill confirmed it was no coincidence.

"That's a subject that's disheartening and unfortunately, I don't think the punishment really fits the action," the 37-year-old pitcher said of Commissioner Rob Manfred's decision to suspend Gurriel for the first five games of next season, keeping him eligible for the Series. "And I think that, rightfully so, the fans spoke out and understood what was going on. So I gave them their time to voice their opinion."

"Never heard a player booed throughout an entire at-bat here like Gurriel was just booed…again, good," *Los Angeles Times* columnist Bill Plaschke tweeted.

"The Dodgers sure love being back in LA, especially now that the temperature at game time is 67 degrees, not 103, as in Game 1," Tom Boswell of the *Washington Post* wrote before the game. "In effect, that pushes the fences back at least 10 feet and may serve as a slight deterrent to the Astros, who are an even better slugging team than Los Angeles."

The issue was moot for the first two innings. Hill was in command. With two outs in the third, he made a mistake on a pitch to Springer, who powered a fastball into the right field stands to give the Astros a 1–0 lead. Hill got out of the inning when Bregman grounded out to short, but Dodgers fans no doubt realized that he had made the mistake of giving Verlander a run to work with.

Springer had come alive. Since his 0-for-4, four-strikeout night in Game 1, he had homered in all but one game. All four tied a game or put the Astros ahead. "Since last season," the *Houston Chronicle*'s Jake Kaplan observed, "Hinch has fielded questions as to why he leads off with probably his best power hitter. Springer's ability to spark a rally like he did against the Dodgers is why."

In the bottom of the third, Verlander cruised, getting Austin Barnes on a grounder to second, striking out pitcher Hill on a foul tip into Brian McCann's mitt, and getting Chris Taylor on a called strike three. It was Verlander's fifth strikeout of the game.

Hill cruised through the top of the fourth—three up, three down, and Verlander continued to dominate in the bottom of the inning. He got Corey Seager on a fly to left and then fooled Justin Turner on a 92-mile-per-hour cutter for strike three. With two outs, Verlander got his seventh strikeout of the game when Cody Bellinger swung through a 97-mile-per-hour fastball to end the inning.

New York Times reporter Dave Waldstein noted that Verlander was pitching without the safety net that Hill enjoyed. "That is because the Astros are really out of good options in the bullpen," he said. "Everyone is either worn out or ineffective, or both. The supposed closer, Ken Giles, may not even pitch anymore because he has been so bad. Keep in mind that before the game, Astros manager A. J. Hinch said that he would do whatever is necessary to win tonight, including possibly using Lance McCullers to close it out. 'I think if you complicate it and try to manage two games at once, you'll find yourself having two games.'"

In the fifth, McCann led off the inning with a single to right and churned around to third when Marwin Gonzalez doubled past a diving Turner. Hill chose to pitch to Josh Reddick despite first base being open and the pitcher waiting on deck. It worked; Reddick struck out. Verlander also struck out, and after Springer was intentionally walked to load the bases, Hill's night was over, despite having thrown just 58 pitches. In his anger and frustration at coming out, the veteran lefty knocked over a tray of water cups in the dugout.

Fans were unhappy too, although Dave Roberts said afterward his decision to pull Hill was "the pivotal point." He said he felt Brandon Morrow was the best pitcher to face Bregman. "So that was kind of my gut," he said.

His gut was right. With an Astros runner perched on every base, Morrow came in and got the Dodgers out of the jam.

The Dodgers got to Verlander in the sixth. Barnes slapped a leadoff single into left, which brought up pinch hitter Chase Utley. Despite Utley being 0-for-14 in this year's postseason, Verlander pitched him carefully before bouncing a slider and hitting him. Hinch walked to the mound to talk to his battery and infielders, while Taylor waited at the plate. The Dodger leadoff man swung and missed at a 1-and-1 slider from Verlander before lacing into a 97-mile-per-hour fastball. It bounced into right field no-man's-land, allowing Barnes to easily score the tying run and to leave Utley and Taylor in scoring position.

Seager hit a long fly to right that seemed it might leave the park, but eventually ended up as a sacrifice fly in Reddick's glove. Utley scored. Verlander got out of the inning by getting a foul-out from Turner and a strikeout from Bellinger, but he was done after six innings of work.

"What an interesting inning," the New York Times Waldstein observed. "Verlander certainly looked like he had reached his limit. Even the first out—Corey Seager's sacrifice fly ball to right—was hit hard enough to have been a home run in Yankee Stadium, anyway."

"I think when I sit down tonight and really reflect on this game," Verlander told reporters afterward, "the one thing I'll be upset about was maybe falling behind Barnes (2-and-0), but he still didn't hit the ball very well, and that's baseball. He found a hole."

Verlander also said he didn't want to get beat by Utley on what the pitcher described as "a mediocre slider." He admitted he was concerned about what felt to him like abnormally slick baseballs. He couldn't seem to find the grip he needed to get movement on the pitch. Other pitchers, on both teams, also complained throughout the Series.

With both starters gone, Game 6 became a bullpen battle, the Dodgers having the edge. In the top of the seventh, the Astros threatened when Reddick walked to lead things off and Gattis pinch hit for the pitcher. Dodger reliever Kenta Maeda induced a force-out at second. Springer singled, Derek Fisher replaced Gattis on second and then advanced to third on Bregman's flyout to center. With runners on first and third and two outs, Altuve came up, and was swinging away from the first pitch. He ended up grounding out to third to end the inning, with the throw just barely beating him at first. Astros fans couldn't help but notice that Dodger pitchers were doing a great job on Altuve and Correa, who were a combined 0-for-7.

Joe Musgrove came on in relief of Verlander. The right-hander retired Yasiel Puig on a pop-out to short, but Joc Pederson, who has been on fire of late, crushed a 1–2 fastball for an opposite-field home run, increasing the Dodgers' lead to 3–1. Musgrove recovered to retire pinch hitter Andre Ethier on a fly to left and then struck out Barnes to end the inning.

The Astros walked off the field knowing that they had given Kenley Jansen a two-run cushion to work with. No one was surprised when the burly, bearded reliever did his job in the eighth. He got Correa to fly out to left, got Gurriel to pop out to first, and then struck out McCann to end the inning. Mila Kunis and Ashton

Kutcher waved a giant Dodgers flag and pranced atop the dugout to fire up the crowd. Rob Lowe, resplendent in Dodger blue, waved the flag too.

In the bottom of the eighth, the Dodgers threatened to extend their lead. Charlie Culberson led off the inning against Luke Gregerson with a single to left and advanced to second on a groundout by Taylor. Seager worked a full count, but struck out on a slider. With a man on base, Taylor walked, which ended Gregerson's outing. Francisco Liriano came in to face Bellinger, and the 12-year veteran, who was making his first career World Series appearance, struck out the rookie slugger in a tough nine-pitch at bat.

Jansen had a long wait between innings, but the Dodger closer showed no ill effects, shutting the door on the Astros and securing his six-out save. He started things off by getting Gonzalez to pop out to first. He then struck out both Reddick and pinch hitter Carlos Beltrán to end the game, needing just 19 pitches to complete two innings of work. After six games, he was doing Mariano Rivera work, potential MVP work, depending on who won the Series.

"This series was destined to go seven pretty much the whole time," McCullers noted after the Dodgers' 3–1 victory. The right-hander would be starting Game 7 on his regular four days' rest, opposite the Dodgers' Darvish.

"I don't think you practice as a kid for playing in three, four, five games in the World Series," Springer said. "And I know we lost [Game 6], but this is awesome to have a chance to come out here again. We'll see what happens."

In the clubhouse, reporters asked Hinch about his team's "great short-term memory loss all season." Would they bounce back?

"If you carry any baggage into Game 7 of the World Series, then you're certainly misguided with your attention," the manager said. "We will come as positive as ever, ready to play. It is what looks to be one of the most exhilarating games that we're ever going to be a part of. Who can guarantee that you're going to be in Game 7 ever again?"

CHAPTER 16

Astros' Moon Shot

*Astros for @Astros! Good luck tonight in #Game7 from our
NASA astros and staff. #AstrosForAstros #OutOfThisWorldSeries
#WorldSeries*

TWEET FROM ASTRONAUTS ABOARD THE
INTERNATIONAL SPACE STATION.

How 'bout them Astros?

EIGHT-YEAR-OLD MICHAEL WEINER

For the first time since 1931, two 100-win teams would meet in a World Series Game 7. The Series has gone to Game 7 on 39 occasions, most recently the thrilling 2016 Chicago Cubs victory over the Cleveland Indians, the 8–7 extra-inning win bringing a blessed end to the Cubbies' 108-year championship drought.

The Cubs' win ranks among the classics, right up there with the 1991 Minnesota Twins' 1–0 victory over the Atlanta Braves, when Jack Morris pitched 10 shutout innings, arguably the most heroic pitching performance in World Series history. It's almost on a par with the Pittsburgh Pirates' 10–9 victory over the Yankees in 1960, when slap-hitting second baseman Bill Mazeroski came to the plate in the bottom of the ninth, score tied at 9, and powered a pitch over the Forbes Field wall to give the Pirates their first World Series title since 1925.

And then there was Hall of Famer Sandy Koufax—still on hand in LA to inspire and instruct today's Dodger pitchers—retiring 13 of the final 14 batters he faced in the Dodgers' 2–0 victory over the Twins in '65. Or, speaking of the Dodgers, who lost their first seven World Series appearances, there was 23-year-old Johnny Podres shutting out the fearsome Yankees of the Mickey Mantle, Yogi Berra, and Bill Skowron era, making sure that "Wait'll next year" was 1955.

And now it's 2017, and two superb, young teams, evenly matched, each winners of more than a hundred games during the regular season, both with great pitching and a potent offense, meet in Los Angeles for the first Game 7 ever in Dodger Stadium. The Dodgers and the Astros already have played two of the most memorable World Series games ever. Fifty-four thousand fans in Dodger Stadium and thousands watching the big screen inside a gameless Minute Maid Park won't be at all surprised if they witness another.

On a warm fall evening in LA, it didn't turn out that way, maybe because the Dodgers and the Astros had played each other at the cutting edge of stress and endurance for six games, after a long, long season. Maybe because a human being—and a team of human beings—can live on tension's cutting edge only so long. These guys were as emotionally spent as they were physically exhausted.

"I don't know if I had another inning in me," Houston catcher Brian McCann told reporters afterward. "I'm spent. I'm exhausted. This has been just an incredible experience."

"I think we all reached limits that we didn't know we had in this series. And I think you could say the same thing for the guys across the way," Astros outfielder Josh Reddick commented.

Yu Darvish was back on the mound for the Dodgers, and he fared no better the second time than he did the first. On his third pitch to George Springer, the suddenly hot-hitting leadoff hitter lashed a double into the left field corner. Alex Bregman followed that up by hitting a grounder to first that looked like it would be an out, but Cody Bellinger's throw to Darvish, who was covering the bag, went wild, allowing Springer to score. Bregman had advanced to second on the error and, noticing Darvish ignoring him, stole third. His aggressiveness paid off, as he was able to score on a groundout by José Altuve, making it 2–0.

Darvish, who lasted just five outs in his Game 3 start, was able to get out of the inning by retiring Carlos Correa on a grounder to first and winning a 13-pitch battle with Yuli Gurriel, who flew out to right. The stadium was quiet as the Dodgers headed into the dugout. Eyes glanced toward the Dodger bullpen. Was that Clayton Kershaw warming up? Dodger fans wanted to see the tall Texan in the game.

The Astros were relying on young Lance McCullers Jr., but working with a two-run lead he was almost as shaky in the first inning as Darvish. Just like the Astros, the Dodgers started things with a double when Chris Taylor launched a ball to the wall in right-center. Corey Seager struck out, but McCullers hit two batters with pitches. Between the two plunks, he struck out Bellinger and with the bases loaded induced Joc Pederson to ground out to second to end the inning.

McCann started the top of the second by drawing an

eight-pitch walk. Ever-reliable Marwin Gonzalez, in a debilitating slump for most of the World Series, followed with a double to the wall that would have scored most runners, but not the Astros' speed-challenged catcher. With runners on second and third and no outs, Darvish got the first out of the inning on a soft grounder to second from Reddick. That brought up McCullers, who was swinging away rather than trying to bunt McCann home. The strategy worked. McCullers hit a soft grounder to second, and McCann rumbled home. Astros 3, Dodgers 0.

Darvish would last just one more batter. Springer worked a full count before getting a fastball he liked, and then drove it out of the park for his fifth home run of the World Series. Astros 5, Dodgers 0. Back home in Houston, the Minute Maid crowd went crazy.

"I remember my plan and my approach was to get something out over the plate, get something I could drive," Springer would say afterward. "If I was going to go down, I was going to go down on my own accord. And I just remember swinging and hearing the sound of the bat, and I knew it was a good sound. And then I saw the flight of the ball. And I got to first base and I rounded third, and got home and that's a crazy feeling. It's a very surreal feeling, because this is Game 7. This is what you dream of as a kid. And for that to happen is indescribable."

Brandon Morrow, who had pitched in each game of the World Series, and 13 of the Dodgers' 14 playoff games, came in to replace Darvish. He struck out Bregman on three pitches to end the inning.

In the bottom of the inning, McCullers put two more runners on base, but once again got out of trouble without allowing a run. With Logan Forsythe on second, Dave Roberts sent up Kike Hernández to pinch hit for pitcher Morrow; he reached base on a walk. But Taylor lined out to short, and Correa was able to throw behind Forsythe to double him off at second after making the catch.

Morrow's World Series was done. He became just the second pitcher to appear in seven World Series games in a single season, joining Darold Knowles of the 1973 Oakland A's.

In the top of the third, desperate Dodger fans got their wish. Roberts brought in the mighty Kershaw as a reliever, and the ace needed just 10 pitches to get three outs. The left-hander got Altuve to fly out to center, Correa to fly out to right, and then caught Gurriel looking at a 95-mile-per-hour fastball that was low in the zone but high enough to satisfy home plate umpire Mark Wegner. Strike three.

In the bottom of the third, the Astros went to their bullpen as well. McCullers started the inning by giving up a long single to right-center—and then plunked Turner with a pitch for a second time. It was McCullers's World Series record-setting fourth hit batter. He struck out Bellinger on five pitches, but A. J. Hinch had seen enough, sending McCullers to the showers after only 49 pitches. Brad Peacock got the Astros out of a jam, as the Dodgers stranded two runners.

"Gone are the days of Jack Morris and Sandy Koufax going the distance in a Game 7," the New York Times Dave Waldstein noted. "Both of the starting pitchers are gone from this game in only the third inning. This is the first time in a World Series Game 7 that both starters did not pitch at least three innings."

Kershaw got past the Astros in innings four and five, prompting Waldstein—and probably most Dodgers fans—to say that the Dodgers ace should have started instead of Darvish. He opened the fifth inning by becoming the first Dodgers pitcher of the day to retire Springer when he got the Astros' slugger to strike out on a slider up in the strike zone. He struck out Bregman as well, and then ended the inning by getting Altuve to fly out to Bellinger in foul territory.

The Astros' Peacock also was pitching well. Through the fifth, the Dodgers had stranded eight runners. Astros fans had to wonder when the Dodgers would bust loose.

They got their answer in the bottom of the sixth, with Charlie Morton on the mound, making just the second relief appearance of his career and the first since his rookie season of 2008 with Atlanta. The Astros' fifth pitcher of the night got in trouble early. Pederson singled, Forsythe walked, and, after Morton got Barnes to pop up, the Dodgers got on the board with a run-scoring single by pinch hitter Andre Ethier. Astros 5, Dodgers 1.

Superstitious Astros fans no doubt had Kansas City 2015 nagging at them; maybe some of the guys on the field did too. What if bored baseball gods liked reruns?

Morton, known for being calm and unflappable, kept the damage minimal, striking out Taylor and inducing a grounder to short by Seager, which meant the Dodgers had stranded 10 runners in six innings.

The seventh inning opened with the Dodgers' Mr. Intimidator, closer Kenley Jansen, glaring down at hitters from the mound. He got the first out on Springer's long fly ball to center that a sliding Taylor was able to snare. He struck out Bregman on seven pitches but walked Altuve, who got Houston's second stolen base of the Series by taking second on a first-pitch ball to Correa. That's where he remained when Correa popped out to short.

Into the eighth, and now it was close. Oh so close. A team of 20-somethings representing a 56-year-old franchise had entrusted its fate to a 34-year-old veteran known more for his debilitating injuries over a nine-year career than for his victories. Morton had had left hip surgery in 2010, Tommy John surgery in 2012, and right hip surgery in 2014. In 10 seasons, he had never reached 30 starts or 175 innings. It could get a guy down, for sure.

Astros pitching coach Brent Strom told the *New York Times* that Morton in seasons past had a pessimistic streak and needed to build his confidence. He didn't seem too happy being Charlie Morton, Strom intimated.

"For some people, it's like you're down in the cul-de-sac with the basketball hoop, you're in the countdown, and you're dreaming of winning the NBA championship," Morton told the *New York Times*. "Or you're in the backyard and you pretend you're Ted Williams. I'm sure I did that as a kid.

"But then reality sets in when you become a professional. In a way, I think you start to lose that part of your childhood dreams of being part of a great moment. Honestly, I really just wanted to contribute—to help, you know? I wanted to finish the last few years of my career and be proud of it and feel like I did a good job."

Still, the Astros saw something the naked eye can't see, but high-powered video equipment can. The spin rate of his pitches told them that if he would throw more curves and four-seam fastballs, and fewer sinkers, he could be highly effective. In this World Series, Morton was proving them right.

He came back out for the seventh and retired the Dodgers' 3-4-5 hitters in a row. He was perfect again in the eighth, so

Hinch—playing a hunch, not the numbers—let him bat in the top of the ninth.

And now it was the bottom of the inning, 3 hours and 40 minutes after the first pitch of Dodger Stadium's first-ever Game 7. The Astros tall, slender right-hander walked to the mound and stared in at catcher McCann, crouched behind pinch hitter Chase Utley. McCann signaled, set his mitt for a target, and Morton fired. The catcher barely has to move his mitt. Again he fired. Same thing. And again. Morton struck out Utley on three pitches. One down.

Chris Taylor stepped in, and inside a crowded, noisy Mexican restaurant in North Hollywood called El Tejano, Bao Chung, 39, of Sugar Land stood near the bar, a mug of beer in hand. He was surrounded by exiled Astros fans, exalted Astros fans. He caught himself holding his breath. He and a friend had bought a ticket to Los Angeles at the last minute to watch Game 6. It was the first time Chung had ever been in LA.

"We lost, but we ended up staying," he told a *Los Angeles Times* reporter. He and his buddy spent the night in their rental car.

Most baseball fans know about packing up the equipment before the last out, or some version of the old baseball superstition. Chung and his buddy, thousands of fans back at Minute Maid, the Dean family in their storm-ravaged home, fans in sports bars and living rooms, in hotel rooms and hospital rooms, in truck stops on the Interstate and prison dayrooms behind tall fences— Astros fans who were glued to a TV wherever they happened to be knew they couldn't start high-fiving yet. Still, this thing just felt right, like it was fated. Could it be those fickle baseball gods were leaning Texan on this night? Could it be the old Judge, looking on from his celestial digs, the only ones that could ever outshine his Astrodome manse, had tweaked some heavenly strings? The Dodgers, down four runs, seemed resigned. They seemed beaten. Didn't they? Fans looked to each other for reassurance.

Morton, who seemed calm in the eye of baseball's hurricane, gathered himself and threw a laser to Taylor. The young man who got the Series started with a first-pitch home run grounded out to Altuve. Two down.

The Astros infield shifted as Seager came to the plate. Morton came set and fired a 96-mile-per-hour fastball. Seager swung and made contact. It was an easy grounder to Altuve, who was in just the right spot. Astros fans held their breath, held their mugs of beer, held their hopes for another 10th of a second. They watched the little second baseman look the ball into his glove, just as he'd done countless times since he was a little kid scuffling barefoot on the hard-baked sandlots of Venezuela, just as he had done for Astros scouts not many years ago. In one smooth motion, he took the ball out of his glove, threw over to Astros first baseman Gurriel and it was over. Over! The 33-year-old rookie from Cuba, brand new to this country, threw his arms atop his head in joy and disbelief.

McCann, who caught Morton's debut for the Atlanta Braves in 2008, jumped into the pitcher's arms to celebrate. Springer, who soon would be named the Willie Mays World Series Most Valuable Player, raced in, arms waving, from Willie Mays territory, center field, to join the scrum. Altuve leaped into Correa's arms. The young shortstop—shortly before a personal date with destiny—waved a Puerto Rican flag, his joyful island buddies Carlos Beltrán, Juan Centeno, and about-to-be-Red-Sox-manager Alex Cora gathered around him, embracing. The jubilant Astros on the field were a long way from Florida in February, when their incredible journey began.

Bregman was almost overcome. "I just dropped down to my knees and realized a childhood dream came true," he said afterward. "This team worked so hard for this. It's so special to be a part of this team. The coaching staff is unbelievable, ownership, our general manager, the city of Houston. We won this for them."

They knew it. Inside Minute Maid, where the decibel level was as high as if the Astros were winning at home, watch-party fans leaped and hollered and hugged. They exchanged hearty high-fives with strangers. Orbit, the Astros' mascot, unveiled a big, new flag—orange with white lettering that spelled out "World Series Champions 2017."

"This very well may be the very greatest Houston sporting moment in the history of this city," 38-year-old David Weiner told Ben DuBose of MLB.com. Weiner was attending the Minute Maid watch party with his wife, Stacy, and son Michael, 8.

While the craziness of the Astros' clubhouse showed on the jumbotron—champagne-soaked players in black goggles, players hugging, toasting each other, lighting up big cigars—Weiner talked about his own family's experience. Like so many other Houstonians, their Meyerland home had been uninhabitable for more than two months. When the floodwaters came rushing in, they had to be rescued from the second floor by the Houston Fire Department. For both parents and especially for their son, the Astros' championship run had provided a much-needed diversion. It had helped keep their spirits up.

"He's really gotten into this Astros run," David said of young Michael, a kid with floppy, dark hair. "It's something that has helped take his mind off of everything going on, and it's really given our entire family something to rally around. We're [temporarily] living with my parents, and we can go upstairs and he can watch the game with his grandpa. It's been a very nice and very welcome diversion."

From the International Space Station 254 miles above the earth, astronauts Randy Bresnik, Joe Acaba, and Mark Vande Hei conveyed best wishes to their hometown team.

At a jam-packed Christian's Tailgate Bar & Grill, a popular gathering place in the Heights section of Houston, bartenders danced on tables and waved towels. "Beer is flying everywhere," *Chronicle* education reporter Shelby Webb tweeted. "EVERYBODY IS ON THEIR FEET. OH MY GOD WE DID IT."

Ryan Slattery, the designer who spent days and nights volunteering at George R. Brown Center, watched Game 7 at a Houston bar with several buddies who volunteered with him. At the last out, they spilled into the street with thousands of others. Downtown was wall-to-wall people, like Times Square on New Year's. It was wall-to-wall noise, loud enough for neighborhoods beyond downtown to hear.

"I don't believe in providence, or fate or things that are meant to be, but I got real close after watching Game 7," Slattery recalled a few weeks later. "It was a moment when I just about found religion. It was a moment that just worked out perfectly. It was Houston Strong."

Back in LA, a reporter asked Altuve to reflect on his Astros journey since being called up in 2011. He grinned, put away his iPhone—he was checking his rapidly expanding Instagram account—and recalled the lean years.

"It's a crazy journey, man," he said. "But I think I was the only one in 2011, '12 and '13, those hundred losses, three years in a row. It's not easy. But I kind of like believed in the process. I believed in what Jeff Luhnow and Jim Crane used to talk to me: 'Hey, we're going to be good. We're going to be good.'

"Then, okay, let me keep working hard. Let me get better every year and try to be part of the winning team. Like I always believed that we're going to become good. Then I saw Springer get drafted, Correa and Bregman, and I was like, okay, here we go.

"We got to the playoffs in 2015. Very young team, we didn't have that much experience. We couldn't go farther. But last year we have another great year. I think it was a good year, we didn't clinch, but it was another good year. And then this year in spring training I realized, like, this is the team! It's something in our clubhouse, like a lot of chemistry, like good relationship between players, coaches, players with everybody, and I was like, okay, I kind of like believed it was the year. Everybody did it, and now we're here."

Meanwhile, Altuve's infield buddy was still on the field, busy with a matter more urgent than answering reporters' questions. The irrepressible Carlos Correa asked his girlfriend to marry him—on national TV. He told his teammates before the game what he was planning to do—if the Astros won—and he entrusted the ring to the clubhouse manager. With the Astros leading in the ninth, he asked for the ring.

———————

At the conclusion of an interview with Ken Rosenthal of Fox Sports, Correa drops to one knee, opens the little velvet box, and holds the gleaming ring toward his girlfriend. Her hands fly to her face in shocked surprise.

"And right now I'm about to take another big step in my life," the tall, young man recites nervously—you can imagine him rehearsing before a mirror at home—as friends and family members look on. "Daniella Rodriguez, will you marry me?"

An emotional Rodriguez, Miss Texas USA in 2016, moves past a waist-high barricade to embrace and kiss Correa. He places the ring on her finger.

She says yes.

Back in Houston, eight-year-old Michael Weiner was still up, still celebrating with thousands of other fans.

"How 'bout them Astros?" the youngster said, a big grin on his face. "This has been the best night of my life."

EPILOGUE

A year that began with Houston enthusiastically hosting thousands of football fans and partygoers in town for Super Bowl LI at NRG Stadium—New England Patriots 34, Atlanta Falcons 28—rolled toward its end with a rollicking downtown parade on a glorious November morning, a morning that felt like the happy merging of summer and fall for a city that knows what it's like to be pummeled by the weather. Houston was hosting its first victory parade since the celebrations honoring the NBA's Houston Rockets in 1994 and 1995.

Four NASA T-38 jets piloted by astronauts soared over a sea of orange and blue along the 29-block parade route. More than 750,000 jubilant fans—including school kids officially off for the day—lined streets that had been flooded just nine weeks before. They had come downtown to welcome the World Champion Astros. They hung out of multilevel parking garages and office buildings, watched from the limbs of trees along the parade route and screamed with joy when José Altuve, George Springer, Carlos Correa, Alex Bregman, and the rest of the guys rode through a blizzard of confetti fluttering down from skyscrapers. The Astros screamed back and happily showed off the 30-pound sterling-silver trophy they had brought home from LA. A woman held up a sign that checked off the year's triumphs: "Beat Boston. Beat New York. Beat LA. Beat Harvey."

Maya Wadler, the teenager whose family had been flooded out of her home, was on hand for the parade. She had missed so much school that her principal refused to allow her to accompany her fellow seniors on a long-anticipated trip to Israel. She had gotten the devastating news that morning. She and a couple of friends drove downtown and scooted to the front of the crowd to get a close look at their heroes. The joy of the moment helped her forget her disappointment about the trip.

"Everyone was so happy," she said. "No one was upset, even though you know they've been through hell." (Later, her father took her to Israel; the family hoped to get back into their home by April.)

"We're at the point in Houston where you could punch someone in the face and they'd hug you as long as you yelled 'GO ASTROS!'" Robert Downen tweeted the morning of the parade. (Even a guy in a Halloween chicken suit might have felt magnanimous.)

Springer thanked Houston for sticking with him through good times and bad. Brash outfielder Josh Reddick, a fanatical WWE fan, channeled Ric "The Nature Boy" Flair and his trademark "WOO!!"

Reddick, a wide WWE championship belt slung over his shoulder, greeted the joyous crowd gathered around the reflecting pool at City Hall. "WOO-ston," he yelled. "We don't have a problem. We have a championship!"

Many in the crowd wore newly purchased Astros gear or necklaces featuring a medallion that read "Earned History," a play on the team's "Earn It" motto. Others waved copies of the *Houston Chronicle* that had hit the streets within minutes of the Game 7 victory. The huge headline read "Champs."

Only once before had I seen hundreds of people line up day after day to buy a newspaper. That was in Washington, when for days after President Barack Obama's 2008 election, people waited in line on 15th Street outside the *Washington Post* to buy a copy of the newspaper's front-page stories about that historic event.

I saw it again at the *Chronicle*, with people queuing up day after day to buy the "Champs" edition at a pop-up shop in the parking lot. The *Chronicle* initially printed 125,000 copies, then another 150,000 copies overnight, and then finally 250,000 copies.

A few days after the parade, the magnificent Altuve was named the American League's Most Valuable Player, the five-foot-six-inch second baseman outpolling the six-foot-seven-inch New York Yankee slugger Aaron Judge. Altuve appeared on *The Tonight Show* and *Saturday Night Live*, shortly before *Sports Illustrated* named him "Sportsman of the Year" (along with the incomparable J. J. Watt for his charitable efforts post-Harvey). The Associated Press named him "Male Athlete of the Year."

At a sporting goods store in the Houston suburb of Katy a few weeks after the season, fans began lining up at midnight to get Altuve's autograph when the doors would open hours later. Some had tears in their eyes when they approached the 27-year-old superstar. As the *Houston Chronicle* reported, some wanted to tell him how they had grown up watching the Astros and how much he and his teammates had meant to them during Harvey.

Those fans understood the Astros' significance to Houston and southeast Texas, even if they hadn't read what Altuve told *Sports*

Illustrated after visiting the people who had sought shelter in the George R. Brown Center when it looked like Harvey was winning. "I saw a lot of people there who told me they lost their homes, lost everything they had," he said. "I felt bad. But in the middle of all that disaster we were able to still see smiles on their faces. I said to myself, 'These people are going through a really tough time, and they're still able to smile. And you're able to give them hope.' That's what it's all about, helping each other."

The Houston Astros weren't the first sports team to inspire their city during a time of crisis. The New Orleans Saints after Katrina. The Boston Red Sox after the 2013 marathon bombing. Also the San Francisco Giants and the Oakland A's, neighboring teams that buoyed the Bay area when the Loma Prieta earthquake hit just minutes before the start of Game 3 of the World Series at the Giants' Candlestick Park. The Series was postponed for 10 days, and residents welcomed the teams back as a distraction from heartache and the tedious task of cleaning up.

So, there were precedents, but it's safe to say that no city took a team to its heart during great difficulty the way Houston embraced the Astros. And vice versa.

Astros fans could take heart in the prediction that the team was set for an extended run. Their Core Four, the first four batters in the World Series lineups, were all young and slated to stick around a while. As the '18 season loomed, Bregman and Correa were just 23. Altuve, 27, wouldn't be a free agent until 2020, Springer in '21, Correa in '22, Bregman in '23. Twenty-four-year-old Derek

Fisher, highly regarded and highly talented, soon would be joining the mix.

The Astros pitching staff likely would be stronger than ever. GM Jeff Luhnow made a couple of midwinter trades to buttress a sometimes shaky bullpen and also pulled off a trade with the Pittsburgh Pirates for former All-Star right-hander Gerrit Cole. A 19-game winner in 2015, the 27-year-old has one of the best fastballs in the game.

Astros co-ace Dallas Keuchel had offseason surgery on his foot and was poised for a stellar, injury-free season. Charlie Morton and Lance McCullers Jr., both revived and rejuvenated after their postseason performances, would be back. McCullers wouldn't be a free agent until 2022. Twenty-year-old Forrest Whitley, who stands six feet seven inches and struck out nearly 14 batters every nine innings in the minors in 2017, could be a budding Randy Johnson. And, of course, there was the superbly talented Justin Verlander, who would likely be one of baseball's premier pitchers for at least another couple of years, maybe longer.

It took the Astros years to get to the top; staying there could be harder—despite the positives on the field and off. The analytics model is in place and functioning the way Luhnow envisioned when he arrived in Houston; its success, however, means that high draft choices are no longer available.

Success also breeds imitation. A number of teams adhering to the Astros model—the Padres, the White Sox, the Phillies—are on their way up. The Cubs, the Yankees, and the Dodgers already flirt with peak performance.

"We're going to have to learn to handle success equally as well, if not better, than we handled the failure when we first got into this," A. J. Hinch told reporters shortly after the Astros won the World Series. "That, to me, is one of the most exciting challenges."

However daunting that challenge might be, the *Sports Illustrated* seers who made their bold prediction in 2014 peered into their tea leaves again and saw an Astros repeat for '18.

"The road will get rougher...[b]ut the Astros are the kings, and they're unusually well-positioned to hang onto the crown even as all those usurpers come for them," wrote Ben Reiter, shortly after the Series. "It all goes back to Springer. He was the seed from which all of this bloomed."

And Houston itself? A seer for the nation's fourth-largest city would likely conjure a mixed future for this growing, dynamic, and diverse community. In fact, it doesn't take a seer to envision both great promise and daunting challenges.

Three months before Hurricane Harvey hit southeast Texas, Harris County began its "Countdown to the Start of 2017 Hurricane Season," with hurricane-awareness messages on billboards and broadcast and social media. Harris County Judge Ed Emmett reminded Houston-area residents "to be alert, because the region can be hit at any time."

Emmett's message seems long ago. As an incredible year ended, Houston and Harris County still were trying to cope with an estimated $298 billion in damage, with thousands of people still displaced. Those men, women, and children Altuve met at the GRB in September moved on after a few days to a motel or subsidized apartment, a FEMA trailer, perhaps to a relative's residence, but as the year came to an end, many still could not return to their homes. Many never will be able to.

Some Houstonians will continue to need therapy and extended medical care to aid recovery. Charity dollars and federal funds will be needed far into the future. Businesses, particularly small businesses, remain shuttered. Houston's downtown arts district, including its renowned Alley Theatre, Houston Ballet, Houston Symphony, Houston Grand Opera, and Society for the Performing Arts, sustained serious damage from bayou flooding.

Those losses are among the everyday concerns of a city slowly returning to normal, of residents getting back to work, rebuilding their lives, looking after their children, trying to navigate complicated insurance forms, FEMA documents, and contractors' red tape. (An abnormally cold stretch of weather at year's end, complete with a rare scattering of snow and ice, only added to the bother).

For public officials—indeed, for all of us—the challenge is to focus on protecting the city from future Harveys. Over the years Houstonians have talked about respecting the environment and erecting barriers to the danger of storms and floods, but somehow we never get around to doing what needs to be done. We have aided and abetted the development of a sprawling, freeway-dependent city built on a boggy prairie next to a storm-prone sea. For eons, the prairie helped absorb rain water. Now, much of that once-open land is slathered over with massive subdivisions, strip malls, and miles and miles of impervious roads and parking lots—relentless development that paves over Mother Nature's method for dealing with floods.

Houston's reputation for no-zoning, no-holds-barred development is an exaggeration, although it's accurate enough to suggest what needs to be done. The question is whether Harvey will be the storm that finally triggers foresight. Jim Blackburn, an environmental lawyer associated with Rice University, is optimistic that it will.

Failure to act boldly, he argues, could imperil Houston's growth and prosperity. The Astros' Verlander may be willing to cast his lot with our city, but worldwide images of a paralyzed metropolis, with terrified residents plucked from rooftops by rescuers, is not the kind of publicity that will attract new employers or employees. Business and industry with plans to expand might be inclined to look elsewhere.

"This is the time," Blackburn says, "that we can make or break the future of Houston."

As a *Houston Chronicle* editorial writer and columnist, I've written regularly about what this city needs to do about the challenges of wind, rain, and water, about the need for resilience and responsible development. I've also written more recently about what Hurricane Harvey revealed about this city's people. Houstonians young and old, native and new, learned they were stronger and more resilient than they might have expected. They discovered wells of compassion and kindness in themselves and their neighbors they might not have known about. At a moment of crisis, they did themselves proud.

This roiling, raucous city's spirit, its generosity, its strength as Harvey pummeled the place reminded me of an early-day Houstonian who had her own experience with floods, danger, and hardship. Her name was Dilue Rose, she was 11 years old and she lived with her family on a farm in what today is the Houston suburb of Stafford. I wrote about her in a couple of my "Native Texan" columns.

During a cold, wet spring in 1836, the Rose family was among several thousand frontier Texans fleeing the Mexican army under General López de Santa Anna. The army was on the move, sweeping eastward across Texas, intending either to kill or drive out every American colonist in the newly declared Texas Republic. In raw, little villages and isolated farms, the cold and constant rain only added to the misery the Rose family and other settlers were enduring as they faced their own annihilation. They had received word that the Alamo had fallen, all its defenders slain. Soon they would learn, to their horror, that more than 300 of Colonel James Walker Fannin's men in Goliad had been marched out and shot to death on Palm Sunday.

Texians—as they were known in those days—were terrified, their panic heightened by the fact that women and children had been left alone and defenseless, their men either slaughtered at the Alamo or at Goliad or off somewhere with General Sam Houston's ragtag army on the run.

Those in Santa Anna's path, Anglo, Tejano, or African American, did what you and I would have done, what any sensible person would have done. They packed up whatever pitiful belongings they could and fled eastward toward Louisiana and the protective arms of Uncle Sam. Their mass exodus came to be called the Runaway Scrape ("scrape" as in scrap or fight).

Young Dilue, living with her parents, Dr. Pleasant W. Rose and his wife, Margaret, and her siblings, made bullets for the Alamo

defenders and fled with the family across the rain-swollen Trinity
River shortly after receiving word of the mission's fall.

"We left home at sun-set, hauld beding Clothing and provision
on the sleigh with one yoak of oxin," she recalled in a remarkable
reminiscence first published in 1898. (Her spelling and syntax
were eccentric, but her memory was crystal clear.) "Mother and I
walking she with an infant in her arms. brother drove the oxen.
two little sisters rode in the sleigh. we were going two miles where
we could get in a cart. Father was helping with the cattle. he joined
us after dark."

The rain had set in weeks earlier, turning the roads into bogs
of red or black mud. Rivers spilled out of their banks—east of
Houston the Trinity was more than a mile wide—and the lowlands
became impassable swamps. Livestock drowned. Cold, sick, and
exhausted, women and children walked barefoot. Measles, whoop-
ing cough, and fevers of various sorts set in. Babies, including the
Roses' newborn daughter, died in their mothers' arms.

Historian Kate Scurry Terrell wrote decades after the event of
a group of exhausted refugees camping at a plantation on Buffalo
Bayou on the evening of April 21 after a long slog in a cold rain.
"Towards sunset," she recalled, "a woman on the outskirts of the
camp began to clap her hands and shout 'Hallelujah! Hallelujah!'
Those about her thought her mad, but, following her wild gestures,
they saw one of the Hardins, of Liberty, riding for life towards the
camp, his horse covered with foam, and he was waving his hat and
shouting, 'San Jacinto! San Jacinto! The Mexicans are whipped and
Santa Anna a prisoner!'"

Until the end of April, the Rose family camped outside the
southeast Texas town of Liberty, where they buried their newborn

daughter. Dilue described how, on their way home, a man named King got his family across a rain-swollen bayou and swam back to fetch his horses. He had gotten nearly across with them, when a large alligator surfaced. The man's wife first saw it and screamed. The alligator struck her husband, and he went under. Several men fired their guns at the animal, but it did no good. Mr. King was gone.

Back home, the Rose family discovered that their house had been broken into. They considered themselves lucky, since many other settlers lost everything, either to looters or the Mexican Army. Dr. Rose's bookcase had been ripped apart and hogs sprawled across his books and medicines. Meanwhile, the corn field needed plowing, so he hitched up his oxen and went to work—on the Sabbath, no less—before cleaning out his office.

"Mother was very despondent, but Father is hopeful," Dilue wrote. "Says Texas wold gane her Independ-ence and become agreat nation."

And so it did.

Two years later young Miss Rose concocted a plan of her own that was almost as audacious as Houston's founders, the Allen brothers of New York. Not quite 13 and fearful she would be an old maid, she resolved to dance with President Sam Houston at the second annual San Jacinto Ball. She was almost within reach of the great man that evening when, alas, a "pretty young widow" politely bumped her aside. Dilue Rose—later Dilue Rose Harris—settled for a Texas Ranger. She was 14 when they married.

Whether Dilue Rose Harris was a baseball fan, I have no idea. She lived into the 1890s, when every Texas town large and small had a team. Houston had the Babies, so named because they were the last team to join the newly formed Texas League in 1888. Who knows, maybe she saw the Babies play. Maybe she would have been an Astros fan had she lived a century later.

What I do know in the wake of Hurricane Harvey is that the grit and gumption of Dilue Rose Harris lives on. During a time of danger, trouble, and turmoil, she was Houston Strong. So are today's Houstonians, who refused to give way to the ravages of a mighty storm. That badge George Springer and his Astros teammates wore during an unforgettable year is of long and honorable vintage.

ACKNOWLEDGMENTS

*H*urricane Season owes its origin to my agent, Jim Hornfischer, who not only looks after his writers' interests, but pens superb military histories of his own. He also is a very tall guy, which to me symbolizes his far-seeing and perceptive view of all things literary. He recognized that the confluence of Houston's encounter with a monster hurricane and the Astros' soul-stirring World Series triumph was a story worth telling.

"Can you do it?" he asked when we happened to run into each other at an Austin reception for the Texas Book Festival.

"Yes!" I said—and then realized the beastly deadline the project entailed. I knew I needed help, and I got it, beginning with my superb editor at the Hachette Group, Paul Whitlatch, who dealt with our looming deadline with grace and good humor.

I relied a great deal on the *Houston Chronicle*'s award-winning coverage of an incredible year in the Bayou City's history. Any mistakes that crept into the book are, of course, my own.

Thanks particularly to the *Chronicle* sports team, including my friend Dale Robertson, who's been writing and reporting about Houston teams since the 1970s (when he's not writing authoritatively about wine); Astros beat writer Jake Kaplan; columnist Brian T. Smith; the venerable David Barron; and Karen Warren, sports photographer nonpareil. Thanks to *Chronicle* editorial writer and inveterate Astros fan Doug Miller and former Astros executive Jackie Traywick. Thanks also to current members of the Astros' organization who were willing to talk to a reporter despite front-office recalcitrance.

I'm grateful to fellow Houstonians who shared their unforgettable Hurricane Harvey experiences. They personify Houston Strong. Thanks also to public officials who shared, including Harris County Judge Ed Emmett, Harris County Sheriff Ed Gonzalez, Harris County Commissioner Rodney Ellis, and former Houston Mayor Bill White.

My son Peter Holley, a reporter for the *Washington Post,* was a huge help with close editing and creative ideas.

Most of all, I'm grateful for my wife, Laura Holley, formerly a reporter for the Associated Press and state editor for the *Houston Chronicle.* Despite her often frantic duties as communications director for a busy elected official, she spent evenings and weekends collecting photos, copy editing, and tracking down folks to interview.

Finally, I want to mention boon companion Fiona. She spent most days lying at my feet as I typed, except for one afternoon when *Lassie Come Home* was playing in the other room on Turner Movie Classics. I found her near the TV, answering the majestic collie's communicative barks with barks and howls of her own. When Lassie went home, Fiona came back to me. I was happy to have her quiet company.

Joe Holley
Houston, Texas
January 17, 2018

INDEX

Note: The photo insert images are indexed as *p1*, *p2*, *p3*, etc.